Strategic Fixed Income Investing

Founded in 1807, John Wiley & Sons is the oldest independent publishing company in the United States. With offices in North America, Europe, Australia, and Asia, Wiley is globally committed to developing and marketing print and electronic products and services for our customers' professional and personal knowledge and understanding.

The Wiley Finance series contains books written specifically for finance and investment professionals as well as sophisticated individual investors and their financial advisors. Book topics range from portfolio management to e-commerce, risk management, financial engineering, valuation and financial instrument analysis, as well as much more.

For a list of available titles, visit our web site at www.WileyFinance.com.

Strategic Fixed Income Investing

An Insider's Perspective on Bond Markets, Analysis, and Portfolio Management

SEAN P. SIMKO

John Wiley & Sons, Inc.

Published by John Wiley & Sons, Inc., Hoboken, New Jersey.
Published simultaneously in Canada.

For general information on our other products and services or for technical support, please contact our Customer Care Department within the United States at (800) 762-2974, outside the United States at (317) 572-3993, or fax (317) 572-4002.

Wiley publishes in a variety of print and electronic formats and by print-on-demand. Some material included with standard print versions of this book may not be included in e-books or in print-on-demand. If this book refers to media such as a CD or DVD that is not included in the version you purchased, you may download this material at http://booksupport.wiley.com. For more information about Wiley products, visit www.wiley.com.

Library of Congress Cataloging-in-Publication Data:

Simko, Sean P., 1970–
    Strategic fixed income investing : an insider's perspective on bond markets, analysis and portfolio management / Sean P. Simko.
        p. cm. – (Wiley finance series)
    Includes bibliographical references and index.
    ISBN 978-1-118-42293-9 (cloth); ISBN 978-1-118-47946-9 (ebk);
    ISBN 978-1-118-47945-2 (Mobi) – ISBN 978-1-118-47947-6 (ePub)
    1. Fixed-income securities.   2. Bonds.   3. Portfolio management.   4. Investments.
I. Title.
    HG4650.S56 2013
    332.63'2044–dc23

                                                                                    2012030213

Printed in the United States of America

10 9 8 7 6 5 4 3 2 1

To my wonderful wife for her love and support—Kate, you are my soul mate. Also, Jackson and Ella—remember that there are no roadblocks in life, just detours. Always reach for the stars. I love you guys.

A journey of a thousand miles begins with a single step.
—Lao-tzu

Contents

Preface

Fixed income investing is usually looked at as the redheaded stepchild of investing. If even given the time of day, most investors provide it little love, if any at all. What every investor needs in order to construct a solid portfolio is a road map to navigate through the turbulent and stable times, avoiding the black hole of the fixed income world. With over 16 years in the asset management industry, I have navigated successfully through the gyrations the markets present to investors with the latest being the Great Recession of 2008. Through the roller-coaster ride, there are many lessons I learned that will benefit investors, helping them to gain success when analyzing the economic climate and investing their fixed income portfolio.

This book is to help you, the investment professional and sophisticated investor, benefit from the lessons this institutional asset manager learned and prepare yourself, your fixed-income portfolio, and strategy against whatever may lie ahead.

Acknowledgments

I would like to extend my gratitude and appreciation to my industry colleagues who have challenged and supported my decisions throughout my journey. In particular, I would like to thank SEI for providing me the opportunity for professional growth. Finally, to my wife and family, for enduring the time I dedicated to this endeavor and my career: thank you.

One

The Investing Environment

The first section of this book paints the picture of the recent market environment. Similar to a screenplay, the characters and players are introduced. Once the stage is set, I will walk you through the various scenes that have captured investors' attention and, at times, have created numerous headaches for fixed income portfolio managers.

It is fair to say that the challenges asset managers face have changed over the past decade. Although there were some previously seen headwinds, the time period from 2005 through 2011 brought on numerous conflicts that investors could not have imagined.

I will take you along a journey highlighting the necessity to remain on top of the ongoing changes and evolve with the market. Although the market is not a living and breathing entity, more times than not, it gives the appearance that it is. This is felt by those participants who are engaged in its daily activities, who ride the ups, downs, highs, and lows in an attempt to outpace its returns.

CHAPTER 1

Expect the Unexpected

*To succeed, you will soon learn, as I did, the importance of a solid
foundation in the basics of education—literacy, both verbal and
numerical, and communication skills.*

—Alan Greenspan

I t's 5:30 A.M. on Monday, September 15. The year is 2008. I am already
on my third cup of coffee and riding on—at most—about eight hours of
sleep since Friday. I'd spent the weekend glued to the television, watching
the story unfold while strategizing my next move. I remember the day as
if it were yesterday, sitting in the office, at my desk, staring at my four
computer screens and TV, watching the headlines scroll by stating that
Lehman Brothers had filed for bankruptcy. The stock was worthless; the
company's senior debt was now trading near 27 cents on the dollar with
its sub debt in the high teens. As the situation unfolded, the million dollar
question that nobody knew how to answer was: How would the markets
handle the news and subsequent headlines about Lehman's bankruptcy as
they surfaced? Not only was I concerned about how the U.S. and global
markets would handle the news, but also, how would the U.S. government, the Fed, and central banks around the world react? What would
the repercussions be when the equity markets opened for trading in a few
short hours? This was unthinkable. I asked myself, "How could this have
happened?"

This should have unfolded differently. The government was expected to
step in at some point and throw Lehman a lifeline, as it did when Bear Stearns
had fallen into trouble six months prior and needed help. The government
played matchmaker, assisting JPMorgan with the purchase of Bear Stearns.
The Lehman events that transpired did not follow the "Bear Stearns model;"
unfortunately, that model was the simple notion of investors and the media's

hopes and dreams that clung tightly to government intervention. The dream did not come true.

THE MODEL HAS CHANGED

How could one of the top five investment banks just shut its doors? And not only shut its doors, but do so at an amazing speed. As reality set in over the subsequent trading days, it was becoming clear that the investment bank model had changed—and so had Wall Street. I had always viewed Lehman Brothers as one of the top five pure investment banks. Goldman Sachs, Merrill Lynch, Bear Stearns (before they fell and were purchased by JPMorgan), and JPMorgan rounded out the group. This list was quickly reduced to two. First, through the fire sale purchase of Bear Stearns by JPMorgan, and then, with the bankruptcy of Lehman Brothers, the reductions commenced. Shortly thereafter, Merrill Lynch struck a deal to be purchased by Bank of America, impacting the investment community once again. In the end, out of the original five, only two remain stand-alone entities with some sort of resemblance to pure investment banks.

From a technical perspective, the true investment bank breed is no longer. It is extinct. Why didn't the government attempt to save this company as it did with Bear Stearns? Didn't the government know or realize the implications? That question can be answered with ease. It is a simple no!

The investment banks that were left standing eventually converted to banking institutions. There was one simple reason for the conversion: The transformation provided them the ability to receive cash injections if needed. This is vital to many financial institutions in order to help fulfill the overnight funding requirements. Overnight funding is essential for financial institutions—in particular, investment banks—to support ongoing daily business. The catch in making this transformation—and there always is a catch—is that the lifelines or cash injections to help bolster the company's ailing balance sheet are from the government. Therefore, the government will, to some degree, have its hand in the business. If nothing else, its presence will be felt through added regulation. The invisible hand of the government has just become more visible.

LESSONS LEARNED

There were numerous lessons learned over the course of time, including the prior example of how quickly a company may shift from a going concern to going out of business. What differentiates top asset managers from the herd is that they learn from the lessons while the others do not. This holds very true within the world of investing. As far back as there are documented records, there are situations and examples providing lessons to learn. Don't worry; you don't have to dust off the history books or travel back that far to gain insight and for examples to surface.

To start, go back a decade or two and look at the bursting of the technology bubble. It provided some straightforward lessons. At one point in your life, someone (possibly your parents) told you, "Don't put all your eggs in one basket." Sound familiar? If you translate that statement into financial jargon, it would read, "You had better diversify your portfolio to reduce risks." This advice could potentially have saved portfolios—from pension funds to college savings accounts—millions upon millions of dollars, helping to mitigate losses when the markets turned south.

Since the bursting of the technology bubble, investors have navigated through unthinkable events such as terrorist attacks, corporate corruption, and mismanagement at various companies such as Enron, WorldCom, and even Freddie Mac. All these events impact markets, the investor psyche, and ultimately, the way individuals invest. We have also witnessed and lived through a recession in 2004, tied with a jobless recovery and what many call a near miss on a depression-type event with the popping of the mortgage market and structured securities sector a few short years later. This depression-like event changed the investment banking system and the Wall Street landscape forever.

The collapse of Bear Stearns and Lehman Brothers will never be forgotten. I have close friends and colleagues whose hard-earned life savings (in the form of company stock) were washed away in seconds. They were instantly unemployed in one of worst financial job markets in history. In one weekend, Bear Stearns went from a thriving company to just a memory and an asset on JPMorgan's books.

The crisis didn't affect only Wall Street and the individuals employed and living in the financial capital of the world. The crisis also hit Main Street and investors located all over the world; lifelong veterans and those who were right out of business school. The chain of events impacted everyone. This was reality, and it was overlooked by the media and government when headlines were written. This was just the beginning.

FROM BAD TO WORSE

It went from bad to worse. The day following Lehman Brothers' downfall, the Reserve Fund, the first money market fund created, notified investors that it had to close its doors, due primarily to its exposure to Lehman Brothers and securities it held within the financial sector. The fund's portfolio no longer traded "at the buck"—money market lingo meaning that each share was not worth one dollar anymore. The buck is the one trait a money market fund lives and, in this case, dies by.

The premise of a money market fund is that an investor deposits one dollar and at any time he or she is able to take a dollar out. Investments in a money market fund, prior to the closing of the Reserve Fund, were always revered as safe. In some instances, investors viewed money market funds as the next safest investment to a bank account. In any event, the shares of the Reserve Fund were worth less than the prior day's value due to losses from the collapse of the financial markets—usually a characteristic of a much riskier investment.

Most investors, if not all, want to forget exactly what happened, but it will take years, if not generations, for that to happen. With what seemed like crisis after crisis, economic and otherwise, the markets felt as if they never regained their true footing. There are many lessons to be learned from the credit crisis that started in 2007 and the events that helped shape the landscape following the initial downturn. When embraced, these lessons are life changing. Investing through the markets and reliving the events that unfolded from 2007 through 2009 will help define the type of investor that you are.

CHAPTER 2

Navigating through Troubled Water

I've learned that mistakes can often be as good a teacher as success.
—Jack Welch

T oday's market is not yesterday's market. It is a simple statement, but it holds many implications. It cannot be stressed or said enough. Current markets hold a plethora of new and unique securities that are constantly evolving. Many of today's securities were not even available to market participants at the turn of the millennium. Adding to the complexity is the recent government intervention that has shaped the markets with regulation. Increased regulation creates a market environment that is in continuous flux, transforming and molding investor decisions as well as handcuffing them at times.

If, one morning, as you were scrolling through the early headlines you had read a prediction, made with one hundred percent certainty, that the U.S. government and its sovereign debt—such as Treasury securities—would lose its triple-A rating, would you have believed that it could happen? These are the Treasury securities that are 100 percent guaranteed by the government and categorized by every textbook and model as risk free.

What type of probability do you think most investors might have placed on the likelihood? Would you have placed a 5 percent probability on the occurrence? How about 10 percent, 50 percent, or maybe even more? Some might even have said that there is a better chance of winning the lottery. Realistically, most individuals, unless cynical in nature, would have said the odds were low. In the end, in a time of uncertainty and market turmoil, or in this case a staggering deficit, the odds of a downgrade resulting in the United States losing its triple-A rating started to increase. It doesn't matter that the United States is the largest economy or that the United States is a democratic nation. However you slice it, irrespective of the surroundings, the odds should have been low for a downgrade.

DEBT CEILING

The politicians didn't seem to show concern about how a downgrade might disrupt the current economic recovery or what the impact might be if there were to be an actual default. The discussions within the U.S. Congress intensified during late July and early August of 2011 in efforts to find some inkling of common ground or accord between parties on how to move forward and raise the U.S. debt ceiling—which they finally did.

To clarify, the debt ceiling is the maximum legal amount that the U.S. federal government is able to borrow. It is similar to your credit card limit. You have the ability to purchase against the card up to your limit without exceeding it. If you do exceed your stipulated limit, the credit card company likely will impose some type of penalty, such as an over-the-limit fee or a notification to the credit agency that calculates your credit score. The government has to follow rules as well: It can purchase up to the debt ceiling limit but not over. This is important, because if the debt limit is reached, the government is not able to borrow or write checks to pay bills. Although the government is required to follow the rules like everyone else, the fact is, we are talking about the government and the rules can be changed. For instance, they can just raise the ceiling. If the debt ceiling is reached without an increase, therefore limiting the availability of funds, consequences could include having to shut down national parks or even miss payments within the Social Security program. If that were not terrible enough, the possibility of the government defaulting on its own debt would be catastrophic. This activity would be debilitating to the U.S. markets and have implications on a global scale. Being responsible for negative repercussions on a global scale is something that the government does not want and can't afford to do. The government did come to an agreement and found a way to raise the debt ceiling.

TRIPLE A: LOST, BUT NOT FORGOTTEN

Although the odds were low, the unthinkable did happen. On August 5, 2011, the United States lost its triple-A rating. U.S. Treasury securities now only hold a triple-A rating from Moody's and a double-A rating from Standard & Poor's (S&P). The downgrade commenced even after the debt ceiling was increased. S&P downgraded the U.S. sovereign rating late in the evening on the Friday after the government raised the ceiling. Truth be told, there had been rumors for a few days prior that the downgrade was in the cards. It can't be said that the rating agencies' intentions were not telegraphed. This wasn't the first time investors heard about the potential downgrade. A few months earlier, S&P downgraded its credit outlook on the United States to negative. This was a warning that echoed through the investing community. A downgrade to the outlook is not the same as lowering the overall rating, just a change in the rating agencies' view. It is a warning sign, a red flag saying to get your act together. The fact that the government did not heed the warning represents how dysfunctional the government can be. Even with the transparency from the rating agencies, everyone was complacent about the possibility of action being taken until it happened.

It is unfortunate that investors even had to consider the possibility that the option of default was discussed. The thought that the United States could default is ludicrous . . . right? Well, not so fast. The United States did default in the past. The default occurred back in the spring of 1979. Many argue that this was not a default, but I view it differently and here is why. The reason many feel that this was not an actual default was that it constituted only a missed coupon payment. In any event, it is still a missed coupon payment. When an investor is expecting to receive a payment—whether coupon or principal, small or large—and they don't, in my mind, that is a default. As one would expect, the missed coupon payment was very small and the government corrected the matter, but it still produced a stir, as well as likely creating additional uncertainty within investors and the markets.

Just as the government did by dragging its feet on a resolution to the debt ceiling, the rating action by S&P created additional uncertainty at a time when certainty was needed. The U.S. economy was in the midst of expanding and facing various headwinds, resulting in setback after setback. To start, the labor market was weak, unemployment was running over 9 percent, and the housing market was struggling to find its footing. The economy was fighting tooth and nail to stay in an expansion mode and not fall back into negative growth. Now the economy was showing signs of improvement, but would the improvement be sustainable?

POSSIBLE, BUT NOT PROBABLE, CONSEQUENCES

If an agreement to raise the debt ceiling had not been reached, the probability of a global disruption would have been high. The unthinkable could have happened. The U.S. dollar might have been challenged for its status of reserve currency. This is possible, but not likely. What the dollar has going for it is

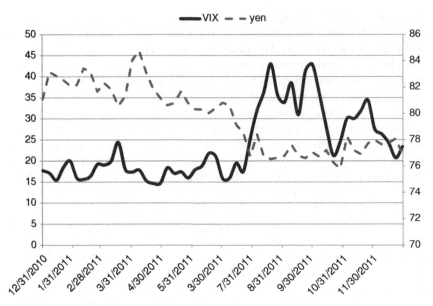

FIGURE 2.1 Appreciation in the Yen when Volatility Increases
Source: Bloomberg data.

that there are not too many contenders ready for the fight. The euro? I think not. There are too many problems and what seem to be conflicting agendas within the European Union to realistically believe that would happen. Even if its financial system wasn't on the cusp of failure, I believe it would be a hard sell to make.

The yen? Well, it has its chances. There is always the flight-to-quality safe-haven bid in the market when trouble on a global scale arises. For instance, take the time period from December 2010 through December 2011 and see how the yen has performed. The right axis of Figure 2.1 reflects the massive rally of the yen versus the dollar. The solid line on the left axis of the chart represents the VIX index, a measure of volatility. The relationship between the two securities is negatively correlated, as you would expect. Statistically, the yen and the VIX carry a negative .77 correlation to one another. As fear and uncertainty gain traction in the marketplace, the VIX index starts to increase its level and move higher. You can see the M-shaped hump from July to September, which represents increased uncertainty. This makes complete sense on multiple fronts. To start, investor fear increased as the debt ceiling discussions—and ultimately the downgrade to U.S. treasuries—were taking place. Additionally, it makes sense that the yen

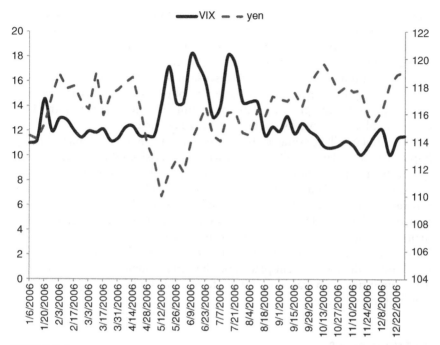

FIGURE 2.2 Correlation Between the Yen and Volatility Remains Negative but Reduced
Source: Bloomberg data.

would outperform the dollar in light of the looming and eventual downgrade to U.S. government debt. At the same time that the VIX was climbing, the yen was rallying off its previous highs versus the dollar. It broke the 80 barrier midsummer and continued on its path to the mid-70s as investors flocked to a safe-haven currency.

Figure 2.2 represents the same two securities in 2006. Keep in mind that this was before the housing bubble popped. Both lines carry a much flatter trajectory. The correlation is still negative, but to a lesser magnitude. For this time period, the two produce a negative .47 correlation. It would be expected that the negative correlation would increase as investors lived through the massive wave of defaults within the mortgage and structured security markets, as well as the changing of the landscape of Wall Street as we knew it.

Even with the unfortunate and devastating earthquake and tsunami that caused the country to practically shut down, the yen held firm. The ongoing battle the yen fights that usually hinders its upside potential is the fact that Japan is a large exporting country, and the government is known for intervening, buying and selling its local currency on a regular basis in efforts to help support the yen. The support can be in either direction—to strengthen it or to weaken it—depending on current levels.

This example was not meant to discuss in detail the future of the dollar and its trading pairs or to predict the future of the greenback. The goal was to help paint a clear picture in the most simplistic terms of why the U.S. dollar is unlikely to lose its status as the reserve currency.

The dollar will continue to be tested as we move forward, but a lasting impact to the dollar is unlikely, even with the massive influx of cash to the system from an accommodative Fed policy and the negative rating action taken toward the United States. There is no doubt in my mind that the procrastination from the governing bodies weighed heavily on the dollar. Post-resolution, the DXY, which represents the U.S. dollar versus other major currencies, shot up, starting a new trend. A relief rally to say the least. The move was short-lived, as the DXY reversed its course preceding the deadline the government placed on the newly founded super committee. This committee's job was to find ways to trim the budget through necessary cuts and to lower the deficit.

WARNING SIGNS

So what do the United States' downgrade and possible default, and uncertainty around the strength of the dollar tell you? In the most rudimentary terminology, it is important to prepare for the unexpected. The nearly missed payment or near Treasury default that took place in August 2011 due to stubborn politicians created the next headache for investors who invest in U.S. Treasury debt. If there had been ripple effects, the problems would not have been able to be resolved quickly.

Today's fixed income markets are certainly different from the markets your predecessors invested in. Those markets, in turn, were different from previous generations, and so on and so on. It can be said that the behavior of prior markets is at times very different from those of today. Due to this thought process, the markets are sometimes looked at as a living, breathing entity with a mind of its own. Sometimes fundamental data points drive the market, and other times technical patterns do. At times, fundamentals and technicals are in sync with each other and other times they are playing tug-of-war. We know that it is not actually possible for the market to make decisions on its own. I do have to agree though, that over my 16 years in the fixed income markets, there were times when the market seemed to have a mind of its own. Continual innovations keep the market breathing. Fixed income markets are more fascinating than equities, currencies, and commodities. In what other market can you create your own security? If someone on the other side of your trade will agree to the terms and characteristics set forth, you have a trade. The market doesn't have set hours to trade. If there is someone picking up the other end of the phone, you can trade.

Although the fixed income market may be perceived as the redheaded stepchild of investing, it is the greatest market out there. The fixed income market is always changing and evolving. It is important to learn from the past; however, remember that the past does not always predict the future.

CHAPTER 3

Lessons Learned

Investing is not nearly as difficult as it looks. Successful investing involves doing a few things right and avoiding serious mistakes.
—John Bogle

Whether you are managing your personal portfolio or managing a billion-dollar fixed income mutual fund, your thought process as a portfolio manager must be the same. It doesn't matter the type of market, whether it is domestic, foreign, or a strategy that blends these and others together. The amount of assets you are managing, either for yourself or an end client, is also irrelevant. The focus, your success, must be centered on your disciplined approach, and most importantly, you must do your homework.

We know that history doesn't always predict the future. What it does do is provide insight that, if recognized, may become very useful.

So what type of information or insight have previous market cycles provided to us? First, back-of-the-envelope calculations show that there is a market turning point, a correction, every 10 years or thereabout. There may be more mixed in, depending on how you define a correction.

Let's go back to Black Monday, in 1987, when equity markets plummeted one Monday afternoon. Next, the dot-com bubble represented the turning point in the NASDAQ as it peaked in early 2000. Subsequently, the housing bubble popped in late 2007 and 2008, once again rattling the markets and resulting in a downward spiral for equity markets. Let me point out that two out of the three corrections were negatively felt within the equity markets. The fixed income markets traded as expected; that is, when the equity market faltered, a flight-to-quality bid occurred and flows moved into fixed income. The most recent correction that carries fresh wounds is the housing bubble, which involved the collapse of structured securities. This correction was different; I would not classify it as equity driven. This correction was fueled within the fixed income world. Unfortunately, equities were not immune and felt the pain as well.

PATTERNS EMERGE

If a timeline is constructed, the pattern that emerges is that a correction occurs approximately every 10 years. The time frame between these occurrences can easily be a coincidence. It also may just be the amount of time it takes for the next bubble to form. If we speculate for a moment, following the ten-year time frame, the next correction may occur in 2018; that is, 10 years from the 2007–2008 correction when the housing bubble broke. The year 2018 is also roughly five years from today, 2013. The potential cause of a future downturn causing the markets to spiral downward can be a wide range of events. The suspicious side of me says the European financial crisis, student loan bubble, and geopolitical events that are occurring in the Middle East involving oil-producing countries are surely on the path that could lead to the next disruption. Not to paint too much of a doom-and-gloom portrait, but there is the specter of inflation and how central banks around the world will unwind all the liquidity and cheap money that was injected over the past few years. My hope is that I am mistaken altogether. If not, let's pray that the magnitude of the disruption will be much less severe because investors around the world have had years to plan and take necessary precautions. In any event, regardless of the cause or the exact timing, the point to glean from the comments is that you should not try to time your investments. Timing or fully moving to cash would be ridiculous. The message is: always be alert. Don't just set it and forget it. Remember that statement well. This saying will come up many times throughout this book. Don't just set it and forget it; set it and monitor it. Look for the abnormalities within the markets and the changes that are occurring within the economy.

Let's revisit those painful days and the effects on the markets with the popping of the housing bubble, which commenced in 2007. A relentlessly appreciating housing market that continued to provide homeowners double-digit returns year after year created the implosion of the housing bubble and market crash. These double-digit returns allowed homeowners to refinance time and time again. In some cases, homeowners continued levering up their personal balance sheet by purchasing homes that were too large. It was the typical want and desire scenario, where the mortgage is too big for the paycheck. Additional downfalls that eventually plagued homeowners and later, the markets, were the purchases of second and sometimes even third homes. This was not prevalent in all areas of the country, but Florida, Las

Vegas, and parts of Arizona were some of the hardest hit areas. There are many possible reasons for this downturn. It is difficult to point to just one problem. Many individuals, including some government officials, try to pin the start of the problem solely on Wall Street. I don't agree with this view. My opinion might be a little biased, but if you take a step back and look at all the pieces, you just may agree with me. Somehow, the media turned the root of this crisis into a battle between Wall Street and Main Street. There is so much research on the cause of the crisis that days could be spent on this topic alone. Movies have been made and will likely be made for years to come. For the purpose of this book, I will touch on different aspects of the crisis, weaving in real-life scenarios and lessons learned throughout the crisis. I will not be covering the crisis in detail.

Broadly speaking, there were two contributing factors. The first factor was all the excess risk and leverage that certain financial companies were pushing for through different investments. Second, and more important, was all the excess that occurred within the mortgage markets, primarily around lending practices. It almost felt as if greed was running wild again. The root of the problem within the mortgage market was with the lenders, who were providing loans to individuals who were not qualified to have a mortgage. Wall Street might have fueled the meltdown due to overleveraged portfolios and balance sheets, but it did not cause the crisis. The lenders and mortgage companies were awarding loans to individuals who were buying too much house and didn't have the income to support the mortgage. Believe it or not, companies were, at times, providing loans with no proof of income. It doesn't take a genius to realize that this type of lending is a disaster waiting to happen.

It has always been the American dream to own a house, and why shouldn't it be? This idea took full hold with the prime borrowers, as well as within the subprime market. The problem was that the lending activity in both prime and subprime markets included the use of adjustable-rate mortgages. Initially this was not a problem; however, when the mortgages started to reset to higher rates after the initial teaser period, some borrowers had trouble keeping up with the increased payments.

So, what happened with all these loans? Were they securitized? This was where Wall Street joined the party. Financial institutions packaged the mortgages and sold them to investors. This was not a new concept. Investors in these securities were primarily institutional investors and suffered as the different types of mortgages, tranches, and securitized products started to underperform. Some of these securities were utilized by asset managers in both the money market arena and other markets. Whose fault was it? That's a whole other discussion. Almost all sectors within the marketplace were affected by the events that unfolded.

MONEY MARKETS

The asset class hit the hardest through indirect exposure from the fallout was the money market sector. If there is a sector or investor that has felt the brunt of the volatility over recent years, it is the short-term investor. There is no doubt that the landscape has changed, and there is a high probability that the scenery will continue to change in the near future. The best way to look at all the change within the sector is through the regulators' eyes. For years to come, the money market sector will continue to evolve, with strength accomplished by creating a solid foundation through added regulation that will possibly change the industry's characteristics.

Money market securities have faced many challenges that continue to linger even four years after the initial malaise. Treasury bills, agency discount notes, commercial paper, time deposits, and repurchase agreements—better known as repos—constitute the lion's share of front-end money market securities. Investors that place money in a money market mutual fund are indirectly subject to these securities. The exposure doesn't end with fund investors. Corporate treasurers use this market and securities to run their daily cash management function. Institutional and retail investors are also subject to the ups and downs of the front-end securities through short-term separate account strategies. The recent environment has impacted all of these securities, some in positive ways and others, unfortunately, negatively.

Short-term anomalies always occur within markets, which is to be expected. For these anomalies to last for years is a tragedy, to say the least. Over the past four years, change has occurred. Change is usually driven by both technical and fundamental characteristics, and over time, the separation or differentiation between these two drivers has converged. The distinct line in the sand is not so distinct anymore, and the water is muddied. In the wake of the financial crisis, in addition to the primary sectors, subsectors of the money market arena were changed forever. For example, asset-backed commercial paper (ABCP) was once a staple in so many money funds and strategies. ABCP helped diversify portfolios by providing new names to managers for purchase. These securities were eligible securities and conformed to the rules and regulations that governed money funds. Rightfully so, there were many programs that carried a solid track record prior to the downturn and to date, still have a solid track record deserving a spot in a money market fund. At the other end of the spectrum, there were tranches of collateralized debt obligations (CDOs) and other more esoteric securities even within the ABCP sector that made their way into money market portfolios. The ability for them to find their way into the portfolio was beyond me and primarily driven by the triple-A rating and enhanced yield that they carried. Many of these securities were overcollateralized with underlying assets, which helped to enhance the securities' characteristics and attractiveness. What this meant was that if circumstances precluded the money borrowed from investors from being repaid, the underlying securities or assets would then be distributed or sold and the cash distributed to investors. Securities structured with the overcollateralized feature were supposed to bring comfort to the asset manager, and ultimately, the end investor. In a normal environment they might have; that is, until they were tested and all parties involved realized that in the middle of a meltdown, the process is not always as smooth as it may sound. In a normal environment, liquidity is not a problem within most sectors, including those within the front end. When the markets showed signs of imploding, though, liquidity was tested. Unfortunately, the tradability of the front end was severely impacted and liquidity dried up very fast. Portfolio managers shunned ABCP specifically, and the securities prices fell. The downward price movement was accompanied by a sharp fall in supply. This was expected, as many of the issuers of these securities were also the large financial institutions that were fighting the battle with their balance sheets due to downgrades and mark-to-market issues. The price action makes sense. Why would an investor want to lend money to a security owned or sponsored by an ailing bank? The sponsor or financial institution providing support to the security was already in the limelight, as investors were frantically trying to calculate which institution might be next to close its doors. In addition, investors and analysts were attempting to decipher which program sponsor had a rescue plan to save its ABCP program. Confidence continued to erode and remained an issue for some financial institutions. In the time of crisis, many found it very difficult to receive funding, even with a strong balance sheet.

When all was said and done, some of the sponsors stood behind the troubled programs, pumping money into them to support their activity. Others looked the other way and decided to let them fail. Many of the sponsors, some of whom supported the programs, were European financial institutions. Unfortunately, there was not a respite for these European institutions. As the financial crisis in Europe escalated, some asset managers were once again deterred from reentering various sectors within the market, including ABCP.

After three years, supply remains less robust than in prior years. The ABCP market continues to feel pain. As hungry money flowed away from this sector, it went right into Treasury bills and industrial or nonfinancial commercial paper. This was a time when the return *of* principal was much more important than the return *on* principal. This concept still arises from time to time, whenever there is stress and strain in the marketplace. Nervous investors who held that view created a strong bid in the marketplace for nonfinancial commercial paper and securities issued by the government.

It took a very disciplined investor to hold true to his or her ideals and process and not be swayed by the enhanced yield available through investing in the financial or ABCP sector. The pickup in yield over nonfinancial or government paper was, at the time, in excess of 50 basis points. That might not sound like too much, but in such an ultralow-yielding environment and for paper with short maturities, such as one week or a month, that extra yield is enticing.

Discipline is another theme that will show up multiple times throughout this book. Discipline is the key to success and will test your process time after time and ultimately impact you or your portfolio.

TREASURY BILLS, THE FAVORED ASSET CLASS

The Treasury sector, Treasury bills (T-bills) in particular, became the asset class du jour even with paltry yields close to zero. The demand for these securities—even with near-zero yields—outpaced agency discount notes, which have the implied support of the government. T-bills remained well-bid through the initial weeks, months, and quarters after the fallout. The risk on trade seemed to have left investors' playbooks. T-bills, which are viewed to be one of the safest investments due to the government backstop and short-term maturity, were again in the spotlight. As noted, this stardom within the different asset classes comes with a price, just like anything else. This time around, the glory was an increase in price, pushing yields to negative levels. If there were any doubts about this status, it was confirmed that, in uncertainty, investors tend to flock to the bill sector. It makes perfect sense that investors will sell risky assets when troubled times arise. This activity is the classic battle between risk appetite and a flight-to-quality trade in the purest form, pushing bills into near-zero and even uncharted negative territory. This flight-to-quality move did not just occur in the U.S. market: The move was much more widespread, touching markets worldwide. Globally, investors were at first looking to shield themselves from credit risk in all shapes and sizes. The risk–reward relationship makes sense. What is unusual is the shift that was witnessed as the equity market started to regain its footing. That is, the risk-on trade was back in full force in the equity markets and now combined with the risk-off trade in the fixed income market, fueling demand in the bill market. It does make sense to some extent that the equity market would regain its traction after the sharp decline in late 2008 and early 2009. Figure 3.1 shows the Dow Jones Industrial Average and the yield of the three-month T-bill from December 2007 through December 2011.

FIGURE 3.1 A unique time when risky assets and risk-free assets rally in tandem. *Source:* Bloomberg data.

The initial move between both of the data points depicts the normal relationship. As the Dow Jones Industrial Average started its steep decline, the yield on the T-bill fell right along with it. There were two questions that everyone was asking: Is the equity market going to find support, or is it actually going to zero? If the markets are not going to zero, what will be the driving force and when will the tide turn? As we know, the equity markets did turn. The final days prior to the turning point, the tone within the markets was extremely negative. The 11-plus hour workdays felt like 20. This was one point in time that I would not have wanted to live a day in the life of an equity trader or portfolio manager. The sense of long hours might have been because there was no escaping the negativity. Once out of the office, on the ride home all you heard about were the problems and difficulties within the market. Comparisons on top of comparisons of prior recessions happened constantly. With every headline, there was risk that a credit we owned and held in a portfolio was next in line for the firing squad.

When the markets turned, it felt like a heavy weight was lifted off. But not so fast. The problem: The bill market didn't follow the expected course of action. The bill market should have started to move higher in yields as the battle was now overtaken by the risk-on mentality. Multiple factors have an influence on the short-term markets in which bills reside. This time, there were four reasons bill rates remained low and did not act in normal fashion as the equity market rallied:

1. Central banks made accommodations.
2. Global growth remained challenged.
3. The global banking and financial institutions were in the process of deleveraging and firming up their balance sheets.
4. Geopolitical concerns continued.

Figure 3.1 shows how the three-month bill remained well bid, almost flat-lining while the equity market marched higher. As a barometer, low T-bills and even Treasury securities are usually a sign that there are troubled times on the horizon. This time around was different, due to the Fed's ongoing efforts that artificially locked in rates at abnormally low levels. Post-crisis, the Fed has provided a quarterly view on when it believes interest rates will begin to rise. This move is geared to provide additional transparency into the market. This activity may continue to hold rates low unless the economic landscape starts to strengthen. The U.S. economy has strengthened since the equity market bottomed back in 2009. The sustainability of growth is what is in question and probably will be for years to come. Working against the positive growth trends in the United States are the headwinds from Europe and sovereign debt risks that just will not go away. Until these headwinds are removed from the picture, the dislocation is likely to persist. The bottom line: Ultralow T-bill levels are not always a sign of troubled times ahead. Granted, we are not in a perfect environment with steady global growth, low inflation, and a healthy labor market. If we were, my expectation would be that the bill market would be moving higher with the equity market. When that time does arrive, driven by less-accommodative Fed activity or stronger U.S. and global growth, the markets should revert back to the norm, removing the dislocation that has been plaguing front-end investors for the past three years and counting.

The contagion effect plagued investors in the midst of the crisis and is now part of everyday investing life. It makes complete sense that if an issuer of debt falls on hard times, the investor base will become nervous, pulling out of the name. In the fixed income world, hard times might mean a couple of different scenarios. A deteriorating balance sheet is never a good sign for a company. This would raise the possibility of a ratings action. Ratings actions within the fixed income world need to be viewed differently depending on the type of portfolio you are managing. For almost any strategy except a money market fund, negative ratings action could be a buying opportunity at a cheaper price, depending on the reason the action was taken. The spread usually will widen out or sometimes may even tighten even on a downgrade. This type of activity doesn't always occur, but it is known to occasionally happen. Here is a great example. If investors were expecting a multinotch downgrade—that is, more than one step lower—and the rating agency took action and only lowered the credit rating one step, investors would look at this as a victory. Depending on how much widening took place in anticipation of a downgrade prior to the event, spreads may now look attractive and buyers may step in. If you are managing a money market fund, it doesn't matter if the current or new levels accurately reflect the rating activity. Different regulations and guidelines do not permit lower-quality debt in the portfolio. Because lower-quality debt is not allowed, sellers will emerge or buyers will go on a strike with that particular name. What that means is that investors will not provide loans or fund the issuer at the current price levels, or at all. In the end, that would put downward pressure on prices, pushing yields higher. That is a textbook example of supply and demand. It is comparable to what happens to those issuers that are facing financial trouble. Worse, contagion may occur, pulling down companies that have stronger balance sheets with those that are under attack. Contagion could also take place by region, though not because of the obvious issues. The ongoing concern about a sovereign default occurring in the eurozone is a reality. There is one positive in this entire situation: the longer the European governments kick the can down the road, the more time all the financial institutions have to mitigate exposure. The bottom line is that these institutions are able to take the necessary measures to shore up their balance sheets and hedge exposure.

Two ways to accomplish this are by reducing exposure or by writing down the value of the debt they own. With that in mind, contagion has to be looked at another way. What really could bring any one of these companies down? The root of the problem is the lack of investor confidence. The fact that investors are losing confidence will likely create a drain on the company's cash reserves, which may impact and erode the balance sheet. We saw this the day Lehman shut its doors and subsequent days during the week. The equity market was falling, and falling swiftly. The financial sector was punished the most, taking the lion's share of the heavy hits. The part that I remember most vividly is that each day, the stock market—the investors within the market—would latch on to a new name and drive that price down. (The shorts would come out, that is, until the government placed a ban on that type of activity.) Anyway, the shorts would come out, and at times, seemed like they were trying to drive the company out of business. The downward trajectory of the financial institutions' stock price spooked many fixed income investors who already owned the debt of that company.

If they didn't already hold a position, they were sure enough not going to put new money to work and invest in a company that was being targeted that day. It was an amazing time, but not in a positive way. Even overnight paper—that is, paper maturing in 24 hours—was not taken down. I was one of those individuals shying away from those names, and rightfully so. The risk was too high. The spiral effect was too real. Balance sheet concerns were not the issue. Markets were moving too fast and too furious. The usual balance sheet woes quickly turned into liquidity concerns, which have the ability to take down a company much faster than the deterioration of a balance sheet.

This is an ongoing theme in today's markets. The run on liquidity or an old-fashioned bank run is a concern today. For instance, if the debt crisis in Europe continues to intensify, financial institutions that have exposure are not likely to go under due to the exposure they have on their balance sheet of sovereign debt. If the entity falls on hard times, it will likely happen because of a run on the bank. The equity market will be falling, driving the stock price of that institution lower and lower. Next will come funding pressure, which is the inability to raise money at market levels. Following that will be signs that investors are removing the institution's name as an eligible investment. You will be able to tell this is happening by the issuing patterns. This is one gauge of how we assess if a company is in trouble. Throughout this entire process the rating agency may still have a top-tier rating on the name. How, you ask? Well, the aforementioned steps could happen so quickly the rating agency doesn't have time to react. The issuing or funding pattern may shift from receiving funding at the one-year point on the curve and slowly moving to shorter maturities. For example, if investors are not buying one-year paper, the company may attempt to issue six- month paper. If investors remain skittish, three months goes to one month, and so on until overnight funding is hard to come by. It is also important to monitor the funding points of an institution. This is accomplished by analyzing certain maturity points and comparing the yield offered that day with yields of the company's peers. For example, if the average for three-month bank commercial paper is 30 basis points but one particular company is paying 50 basis points, you can deduce with high certainty that the company is having trouble finding funding. In all honesty, fear drives markets, and in particular, the front end of the market. In today's environment, this fear turns into the ongoing fear of collapse.

The taxable market was not the only market that felt the wrath of the recession. The municipal market was also under pressure. Ratings were challenged, as were money market securities in the tax-exempt space. It was a challenging time, and without a road map and a disciplined approach, the safe and smooth ride was likely to run out.

MUNICIPALS FELT THE PAIN AS WELL

Municipal bonds are looked at as an asset class all to themselves. At times, this class trades with similar characteristics to the corporate market and other times the Treasury sector. Today, the municipal market has many more similarities to the corporate credit market than it ever did in the past. This is due to a few stark changes and developments within the markets in general over the past few years. Historically, municipal securities have been known for safety and low volatility. Investors were able to invest with confidence that the principal invested would be returned at maturity. Broadly speaking, one reason for this confidence was that states and municipalities are able to raise taxes and in some cases look to the government for funding if needed to fulfill obligations. Additionally, many municipal issues carried what was known as a wrapper. This is insurance from an outside agency to add stability and confidence within the market to investors. In some cases, the insurance wrapper helped the municipality attain a higher rating than it would have without the insurance. There were some instances where the insurance helped the issue receive a triple-A rating. One of the changes alluded to previously is that, in an effort to save money, the majority of municipalities have decided to forgo the insurance wrapper at this point. There are multiple reasons for this decision. For one, the economic climate has changed. Municipalities and states have implemented different austerity packages in order to shore up their fiscal position. As you can imagine, this is quite a daunting task at times. In addition, the fee to insure its debt was enough to curb the prior addiction. Investor appetite was also moving away from the need to have municipal debt wrapped. Driving this move was fallout from the market correction in 2008. Bond insurers over the years started straying away from what seemed to be their core business. Some of these insurers started insuring and taking positions in the structured credit markets. You can draw the conclusion about what happened next. When that market imploded, some of these insurers were hit with multiple claims that now pressured their balance sheets. As a result, their credit ratings were lowered and investors began to fear that the bond insurers that were originally created to provide a backstop to municipal losses were now more a liability than a benefit. This newly attained status as a liability could easily be seen through spread comparison and increased yield. Common sense would tell you that a triple-A insured bond should be more expensive to own with a tighter spread. The exact opposite occurred. Almost all bonds that had an insurance wrapper were treated like bonds on the edge of default. The municipality that issued the debt might have been rated single-A, or even double-A, without the insurance. With the insurance, the rating went to triple-A status, and the bond still traded as if it was a troubled credit.

The stigma of being tied to an insurer was hard to shake. The market was very dislocated. Low single-A debt was trading better and richer than debt carrying a double-A underlying bond that, when wrapped, had a triple-A rating. What was once normal turned into what seemed like an episode of *The Twilight Zone.*

The removal of bond insurance is not going to create turmoil or disorderly activity within the broader market, but how it affects the front end of the investing community is a little bit of a different story. The short-term municipal sector is similar, with its counterpart within the taxable space. Low-volatility, high-quality names are what fund managers fight over. Short-term municipal debt, such as variable-rate demand obligations (VRDOs), is heavily utilized. These securities are issued with a feature that allows the holder to put back the debt at different stipulated dates. In essence, this "put" allows the investor to give back the debt to the issuer. This predetermined schedule may be in the form of daily, weekly, or monthly time horizons. These are just a few examples of the variable-rate demand obligation structure. These bonds are usually triple-A rated. Helping to attain the triple-A rating is the liquidity provider or financial institution that provides the letter of credit to the deal. The letter of credit is usually required because of the put feature. When markets are calm and free of negative headlines, the solvency, liquidity, and creditworthiness of a variable rate demand obligation is never questioned. The problem is that in today's environment, how often do we have a time period, or even a day, when there are no negative headlines or exogenous events taking place impacting investor sentiment? The other problem: Many of the banks providing support through a letter of credit or otherwise are European financial institutions. This concern has grown over the course of the past two years, as the European debt crisis has yet to recede. Some of the institutions providing the letters of credit to the municipal market also find themselves in the middle of the European crisis. The skeptical side of me says that the current situation is starting to carry similarities to the insured market prior to its implosion. The fact that certain European banks have a hand in providing a letter of credit to U.S. municipalities seems a bit out of place. Is the stage set for collapse? Maybe not, but why take the risk? Why introduce a problem that is halfway across the world into a market that is centered within the United States and is a completely different market? European institutions are not the only players; there are other institutions that provide a backstop within the municipal sector. The municipal world is not the place to have European exposure. Why not diversify this risk away? From an investment manager's perspective, it may require them to execute another trade or two. That, however, is their job. By diversifying away this risk, the portfolio manager may also need to give up a couple of basis points in yield—a penalty, if you can call it that,

that is worth taking. There are some who might disagree with my view; as history proves, there have not been too many problems within these securities and sector. Though that may be, we have not had to navigate through the type of events that investors have faced over the past few years. In the end, this is not a risk that I am comfortable having.

AUCTION-RATE MARKETS WERE HIT HARD

Before moving on, it is necessary to touch on the liquidity event that took place in late 2007 and 2008 within the auction-rate preferred markets. There is sometimes confusion about the auction-rate and variable-rate demand obligations. From an investor standpoint, the primary difference is that the variable-rate demand obligation has a built-in put feature, as previously described. The put feature is controlled by the investor. They have control. This is a key difference between the VRDOs and auction-rate securities (ARSs). In ARSs, the investor lacks this benefit. The issuer drives the callable feature. If the issuer is not interested in purchasing the security back, it goes through what is called a Dutch auction process, administered by the dealer community. Prior to 2007, the auction-rate market was functioning. I remember having multiple conversations with different dealers about these securities and why I should purchase ARSs from them. They always affirmed that they (the dealer) would step up and buy the security if the auction failed. It sounded great; however, I am not a fool, and when push came to shove I knew that the broker-dealer would be looking out for only one person, and that was not me. Happily, I was not a buyer, and when 2007 hit and the liquidity crunch in the ARS market was in full force, I was smiling. Securities that were trading one day at 2 percent skyrocketed to 10 percent, and in some cases, higher. There were no buyers to be found. The issuer didn't have the necessary funds to repurchase the debt; the dealer community was starting to have balance sheet issues and didn't want to add another illiquid security to its books. With all the options unsuccessfully used and no letter of credit like the VRDOs have, there was no choice other than falling prices and rising yields. Now, if you were a holder of the debt, at the reset date, you were capturing a significantly higher yield than a few days or weeks ago. The problem: There was no liquidity. If you were needed to access your funds, you couldn't; you were stuck. I took a lot of flak for my skeptical view, but in the end, remaining disciplined paid off. I have never been a fan of these securities. I guess it can be said I have control issues, and not having control over the ability to put the bond back to the issuer was a deal breaker.

CHAPTER 4

Direction in a Sometimes Directionless Market

Success is not final, failure is not fatal: it is the courage to continue that counts.

—Winston Churchill

From time to time over the course of investing, you will find yourself in a quandary. You will wake up, do your routine, have your coffee, and ask yourself, "What trade am I going to put on today?" If you find yourself asking that question, you are asking for trouble. There may not be a lot of opportunities to make money on a daily basis. Early in my asset management career, I would be one of the first in the office, reading the *Wall Street Journal* and *Financial Times*. Next, I would scroll through the headlines across the wire services, check how the foreign markets were trading in the overnight session, get my coffee, and finally be ready to start my day, all before 7:00 A.M. One morning I must have had a look of frustration written across my face. The head of the desk took one look at me and asked, "What's the matter?" He was probably thinking I put a trade on and it was already going against us. I assured him that we were not on the wrong side of a trade, and we were not losing money! He asked, "So what is the problem, then?" "It's quite the opposite," I said. "I am frustrated because I am having trouble finding a trade to put on." He looked at me and laughed, and mumbled some colorful words. The lesson that day was there are not always a lot of solid opportunities to make money. In fact, there are more chances to lose money than to make it. Before I said anything, I stopped myself and thought, "How can that be? We are in the business of asset management, trading and therefore making money." After a few seconds went by, the revelation hit. Although a little bitter, and now carrying a bruised ego because I wanted to prove him wrong, I knew he was right. You don't always have to have a new trade on. In fact, sometimes it is better to have very little on or be neutral to your benchmark. The bottom line is, opportunities need to present themselves and can never be forced. It doesn't matter if you are placing a bond or equity trade or shifting your weights through your asset allocation mix; you need to be patient. It goes without saying that first and foremost, you need to do your homework, and, then, once you have a strong conviction, pull the trigger. I will never forget that conversation. Holding true to the rule, I can say that some of my best trades were trades that were never put on. Remember, the goal should be long-term results, which means investing for the long haul. Only you and the portfolio's investment policy statement can define what that means. To some, it may mean many years. To others, possibly one year, particularly if that is how you are measuring or are measured for performance. Timing the market, you may win a couple if you are lucky. Most likely you will lose more than you ever wish to talk about. Do not try to time the market. Get-rich-quick strategies usually don't work. When you are sitting at a crossroad on where, when, or what to invest in, it is okay. Remember, don't force the trade. As Michael Douglas, playing Gordon Gekko, so eloquently stated in the movie *Wall Street*, "Greed, for lack of a better word, is good," but you need to make sure you know how to harness or contain it. One way is to remember not to force a trade. Not losing money when the market is moving against investors is a win and money making. The markets will test your psyche. You need to use your common sense, and most importantly, be disciplined.

FINDING DIRECTION

A common scenario you will likely encounter over the course of your investing life is questioning the strength or weakness of the current economy. There are many ways to get a feel for the economy's strength. Obviously, do your research—consult the trade journals or financial television shows. Another way is to use your common sense and be observant in your daily activities. For instance, if every car dealer is providing a zero percent interest rate for 60 months, there is a strong chance that cars are not flying off the dealer's lot. Consumers may feel unsure of their employment situation, signaling troubled times ahead. Be careful in your assessment—if only one auto dealer is running a special, it may just be a sign that it is trying to clear inventory. After you gauge the strength of the economy, the next question is, how does the strength of the economy shape the market and its market direction? How do different catalysts affect and shape the market? More importantly, how do they affect investor sentiment? These catalysts have the ability to take on many different scenarios. Comments from the Federal Open Market Committee (FOMC) have the tendency to wreak havoc with investor psyche, especially the statement that is released at the conclusion of the scheduled FOMC meetings held on determining monetary policy and the direction of interest rates. A subtle clue to look for is the number of dissenting voters on the FOMC, along with the reasons for their dissenting votes. Dissenting votes happen for a reason. The definition of the word itself tells the reader that the voters who dissented disagreed with the outcome of the vote. Throughout the years, there have been numerous dissenting members. As with any committee, there are struggles, power plays, and, at times, what seems like a noncohesive group. With turmoil or dissent there is always the risk of losing credibility. Credibility is of the utmost importance to the FOMC; if it is lost, the market and investors will lose confidence, and volatility and wild swings will likely prevail.

Let's take a look back through the 2011 FOMC statements. It is fair to say that 2011 was a pretty event-filled year. The Fed was hard at work, crafting various statements and stimulus to help support the financial system and U.S. economy. Time passed, and probably due to the changing economic and financial landscape, views within the FOMC started to change. There were no dissenting votes in the first four meetings of the year, but the final four meetings were a different story. At each of the remaining meetings, there were multiple dissenters. In 2011, the Fed debated the need for additional policy accommodation. A primary reason for the dissenting votes was that some members felt it necessary to look for additional policy accommodations. The fact that different voting members held differing opinions of the current environment and policy stance not once, but on multiple occurrences, was at times very concerning. It is important to know that there were dissenters at a particular meeting; the key piece that many overlook is why they are dissenting.

A question that should be asked on a daily basis is, when is the bull market within the bond market finally coming to an end? If you have an answer to this, please let me know, and more importantly, let me in on your secret. We do know that since 2007, Chairman Ben Bernanke, head of the FOMC, has orchestrated the rescue of the U.S. economy from what was close to a depression-type environment. He did this through what is known as easy accommodation of monetary policy. One tool he utilized in the battle was to lower the overnight borrowing rate, or what is known as the federal funds rate. He and his committee took this lending rate to abnormally low levels, settling in to a range of 0 to 25 basis points (bps). The Fed's action was undertaken in an effort to bolster not only the economy but also the equity markets and lending markets. What this also accomplished was to lower overall interest rates and Treasury yields to historic low levels. With interest rates at historic low levels, market participants are prepared for interest rates to move higher. So the next logical question is, when will interest rates rise? If they do, how should I position my portfolio? Should I invest in the market or remain on the sidelines in cash until a later point in time? In reality, the answer to that question does not come with a yes or no response. It is a multifaceted answer. The first part to the answer may be yes, as rates hit an all-time low in early 2012. Unfortunately, as mentioned, there is not a simple textbook answer. The direction of interest rates is very difficult to predict, not to mention calling the bottom or highs. Because it is so difficult to predict and there are many contrarian views, rates usually do not move higher or lower in a straight line. A move usually happens in a choppy, directionless fashion. Another way to describe this type of activity is as a range-bound environment. It is just like it sounds. There are two points: one that represents the high and another that represents a low. The price or yield of the bond falls within these two points for a prolonged period of time. Helping create a range-bound environment are headwinds. Headwinds are a thorn in the side of markets and investors. These headwinds take numerous forms and are sometimes difficult to uncover. For example, during an interest rate move higher, optimism on a U.S. economic recovery is normally prevalent, fueling the move. However, a minor hiccup or headwind such as increased government regulation or taxes could create havoc, which is now a distraction. One thing the market and investors dislike is distractions. The aversion for the distractions runs deep because uncertainty is bred from distractions. The aforementioned distraction has the ability to hold interest rates down. It would not be surprising in that case for rates to remain low and in a range-bound environment longer than expected—creating a directionless environment in the near term. Regardless if the Treasury market is moving higher or lower in price, if uncertainty finds its way into investors' minds a flight-to-quality bid will likely occur and Treasuries will rally. This move may be short-lived but it will be strong. A directionless market also can be found within the spread sectors. For instance, investors in the corporate bond sector or agency sector find themselves looking at spreads that are found to be range bound.

Take the time period from late in 2010 to early 2011. The FOMC—led by Ben Bernanke—had, for the prior three years, orchestrated and implemented a plan to stabilize and revive the economy. As discussed before, the overnight lending rate was held in the range of 0 to 25 basis points. Inflation was low, very low; the unemployment rate was on the higher side at 8.7 percent and likely to climb higher. Geopolitical events were surfacing in the Middle East and North Africa, and these disruptions were wreaking havoc on food and oil prices. In addition, sovereign debt concerns were flaring up in Europe. All of these pieces of the economic or market puzzle created the perfect backdrop for a range-bound Treasury market. The nagging question that always comes up at one point or another is, when will the flight-to-quality bid run its course? If you can pick the spot, your year is made. It can be done; it is just very difficult to do. One reason it is so difficult is that whatever turmoil created that bid in the marketplace usually doesn't go away or turn on a dime. There are normally many false starts. Take a look at the current sovereign debt crisis affecting Greece. Every other weekend there are promising headlines trumpeting a resolution to the country's debt issues. New headlines squash the prior week's news as plans change, or in some instances, fall through altogether. It is understandable why market participants become skittish. This type of action is why it is so hard to pick that magical turning point. Here are a few questions that I would consider in the aforementioned scenario when assessing the fixed income market and possible opportunities that lie within:

- To what extent will the ongoing debt crisis in Europe fuel the Treasury market? How much has already been factored in?
- Will geopolitical turmoil and antigovernment protests continue and spread?
- Is the U.S. economic landscape strong enough to support continued growth? Will it be strong enough if there is a default in Europe?
- Is the current FOMC activity strong enough to promote money flows into riskier assets?
- At what point will interest rates rise, or will they fall?

Hopefully, the first two questions will not have to be asked again. For the betterment of the world, I hope that once these problems are corrected, there will not be a repeat of events. But this is probably just wishful thinking, as history has a tendency to repeat itself in some form or fashion.

You can see from the type of questions I have outlined that they could easily be replaced with relevant questions at the time of assessment. The takeaway is that you always need to be thinking, trying to stay one step ahead of whatever situation arises. Don't be afraid to think outside the box. Play devil's advocate, run the scenario through that has a 1-in-100 chance of occurring. You will be happy you did run the scenario when that one chance happens and you are prepared. It will make the decision-making process that much easier.

Two

The Fixed Income Investor

T his next section of the book will help define and build a solid foundation for fixed income investing. The journey will start with an assessment of the different types of investors. I will address the different components and characteristics within the world of fixed income investing. In addition, I will cover the necessary tools to put together a well-constructed game plan on how to navigate through the ever-evolving and changing fixed income world. It is quite important to know what to look for and what should be avoided, and most importantly, how to recognize and have the ability to catch yourself if you are starting to stray from the investment's stated goal.

Who should invest in the fixed income markets? Is it you? Is it me? Once defined, what type of vehicle should be utilized? An argument can be made to hold fixed income exposure in almost every scenario. From pension fund mandates to strategies geared for income distribution, a fixed income allocation is warranted. Ultimately, the correct answer is that everyone– from a high net-worth individual to an institutional account–should utilize the fixed income arena.

Over the years, I have heard many different definitions of what an institutional investor is. A simple way to define this type of investor is by investable assets and investment goals.

This holds true whether you are managing a portfolio for a high net worth individual or an institutional investor. There are certain characteristics that hold a spot within each classification, but in the end, every account should be represented in similar fashion; that is, as a fixed income investor.

There was a time a decade or two ago when there were stark differences between the management of institutional accounts and individual accounts. In this day and age with electronic trading, more fluent systems, and a wide array of fixed income securities, high net worth accounts are able to receive the same quality management and investment strategies that, at one time, only institutional investors had access to.

Regardless of how the end investor is classified, there are multiple vehicles that are available for investment. These include bond funds, money market accounts, and individual securities through the use of separate accounts. All of these investment vehicles provide the necessary tools to meet your clients' end goals. The end result is the same, even as the goal of the investment strategy may be very different. The key takeaway is that all parties' interests are aligned. Their expectations are aligned. This should hold true with longer-term goals and through different investments, such as longer-term bond funds, that will place them on the path.

The goal of a bond fund or a separate account strategy is straightforward; it is the strategy or thesis of the fund. Unless the fund has a different stated goal altogether, the strategy shouldn't be dependent on the end investor.

Ultimately, however the investor is defined, the goals of the strategy remain the same. Short term or long term, the outcome is the same: It's the path you take to get there that may be different.

CHAPTER 5

Define the End Investor

By failing to prepare, you are preparing to fail.
—Benjamin Franklin

First and foremost, one question needs to be asked of every investor, young or old. If you are managing the portfolio's consulting, the answer should be presented through the discovery stage. The question is: What type of investor are you? Make sure this question is answered honestly. Is the end investor aggressive, moderately aggressive, or conservative? At this stage, the view must be much broader. How much do you enjoy watching the market? Are you someone who is glued to the latest financial TV show, pulled into the frenzy of the day, or would you rather not watch the market at all? Remember, it doesn't matter how the question is answered; just be truthful, as this is the core of your foundation that will shape the investing decisions that are made. Sometimes it can be overwhelming to try to accurately categorize your client as an investor, particularly if the end investor is an institution without an investment policy statement. It is important to remain at the broad level, as some investors may not fit with 100 percent certainty into one particular category.

The easiest way to start identifying investor characteristics is from 10,000 feet above. Start very broad and work your way down to the specifics. To start, it is as simple as placing the end investor into one of two categories:

1. Accumulating

    In its simplest form, an accumulating strategy can be looked at as a strategy used for investors saving for a goal. The investor is accumulating assets for a later point in time. There is usually a targeted goal, maybe something tangible that the money or assets are earmarked for, but there doesn't have to be. The goal of an accumulating investment strategy may also be looked at as a capital appreciation strategy. Capital appreciation is attained through investment and reinvestment by trading and active management in which the portfolio receives dividends, coupons, and price appreciation. The strategy will likely have all of the aforementioned activity reinvested.

2. Distributing

As opposed to an accumulating strategy, a distributing strategy is one where assets are removed at different points in time throughout the strategy. The end result doesn't have to be a particular type of account; anything is possible, particularly in this age of customization. The bottom line is that coupons, interest, and even—at times—principal may be earmarked for distribution. Another way to look at this is that the income earned from the portfolio will be distributed to the end investor on a semiannual or annual basis.

One way to achieve a classification is actually to ask another question: Is the strategy income-oriented or does it strive for pure growth from capital appreciation? In this context, income oriented does not mean holding a larger position in the fixed income market when creating your asset allocation. It also does not mean that you are risk averse, which is an entirely different discussion. Here, income-oriented refers to receiving a steady stream of income that is generated from your portfolio.

A strategy that embodies capital appreciation tactics is a different way of describing the accumulating phase. With an accumulating strategy, the rules are completely different. This strategy is also sometimes referred to as a total return strategy. As an investor, you don't have to hold just one classification. The combination of an income-oriented and a total-return investor is possible. With that said, there is usually little crossover between the two classifications within the strategy. It is possible that a strategy may encompass different pieces of each category; however, the overriding goal is a unique occurrence. It is too easy to cloud the water and, as a result, produce a strategy that accomplishes a little bit of both but doesn't reach the end goal. This is like being a jack of all trades and master of none. Whatever your final answer is, the choice will likely be driven by the portfolio's current stage of life or life cycle. The current stage doesn't always drive the decision, but at this broad level it is a beginning. It is not unusual for a classification to also take the form of a moving target. An investment strategy may start out as an accumulation model, but as time goes on, the needs and goals of the end investor—and therefore the portfolio—may change. The difficult part is realizing when a transition has taken place or is imminent. Once the change is recognized, the next step is to act on the realization.

If the strategy is income oriented, it is focused on just that, receiving income. It is very straightforward. Crafting a strategy is not always as straightforward. The strategy will need to be created with the goal in mind to perform well through varying interest rate cycles. More importantly, due to the nature of the strategy, it is paramount that the portfolio be well diversified. You are not concerned with capital gains or unrealized losses. I can't stress that enough. Unrealized losses or the daily ups and downs of the markets need to be tuned out, much like some of the frantic market shows on daily TV. Having the ability to not focus on unrealized losses is extremely important. I am not saying to ignore the potential for losses, just unrealized losses. The nature of the fixed income market will ebb and flow, and in doing so, will create unrealized gains and unrealized losses, and that is all right. What you are looking to do is "clip" the coupon. This is common jargon for receiving cash payments or coupon payments from your portfolio. This is the income that the portfolio will generate. Most end investors who fall into this category use a portion of these funds to supplement current income or as the primary source of income to pay current living expenses. This income may also be reinvested. When reinvested within the current portfolio, additional bonds are purchased or utilized to fund other strategies.

With the growing percentage of population nearing or falling into an income-oriented strategy, a distributing classification and strategy is becoming more widely utilized.

Investors at the other end of the spectrum are not focused on income. These investors' goal in an accumulating classification is almost entirely opposite that of those invested in a distributing strategy focused on an income stream. An accumulating investor should be looking for capital appreciation and outright performance. A total return investor's primary goal is growth; it is not to generate income. Income generation usually occurs in almost any fixed income portfolio; however, it is secondary to the management of a total return strategy. It is almost like an added bonus.

As it pertains to the world of fixed income investing, a portfolio in an accumulating strategy may hold a larger allocation to the high-yield or emerging market debt sectors. These investors may have stickier funds that remain in the portfolio for years. For that reason alone, there is a greater emphasis on growing the portfolio value through price appreciation, which in turn, translates into capital appreciation. As expected, the income aspect of the portfolio is secondary and highly unlikely to be taken into consideration when the strategy is constructed. As with any total return investor, performance of the portfolio is usually measured against a benchmark. This is an important difference. The fact that a portfolio is measured against a benchmark creates a binary result. The portfolio either outperforms the stipulated benchmark or it doesn't. It is black or white, crystal clear. The reality that many individuals forget is that beating the benchmark alone does not guarantee absolute positive performance. The portfolio may outperform the benchmark but still post negative absolute returns or performance. For example, the index may return −8 percent for the year, while the portfolio returns −6 percent. That will be looked at as a spectacular year, and why not? The account beat the benchmark by 200 basis points or 2 percent. However, even though the manager outperformed the benchmark, the bottom line is that your account still lost 6 percent for that year. If the portfolio is designed with an accumulating strategy in mind, this type of result may be acceptable. On the other hand, a realized negative return is not acceptable if the portfolio goal is centered around a distributing strategy. The reason is very straightforward: It may be very difficult to achieve an additional 6 percent to offset the loss of 6 percent. It may never be gained back.

Once the question of the investment goal is answered, the next questions on the docket are how much risk are you willing to take, and what type? Risk in a fixed income portfolio can be very different from risk in an equity portfolio. As with any type of portfolio, there are different ways to mitigate risk. It is sometimes a larger task at hand than initially projected; however, this is driven in large part by the type of strategy. Before we go any further, it is necessary to state the obvious: Risk can be controlled and mitigated if a replicable disciplined process is taken.

The next piece of the puzzle is how you define risk. Once that is determined, the subsequent question is which category does the investor fall into? This is an important piece, as it will help structure the portfolio's guidelines.

RISK

What is risk? There are numerous definitions. The definition below is best for applying to fixed income investing:

> *The fear of capital loss, which includes the inability to receive coupon payments and the return of principle.*

Risk can be easily defined, as the above shows. Every investor, portfolio manager, and risk manager may place his or her own spin or twist on this definition by introducing unique characteristics to feed into the equation. Liquidity, volatility, headline risk, and default are common characteristics that should be introduced in defining risk. Another component of risk that is sometimes overlooked is the projection of future cash flows. This is similar to reinvestment risk, but ties in the specific income needs of the investor with the expected cash flow. A decline in portfolio income can be devastating to the investor. Unfortunately, this is a risk investors have been battling since the Fed embarked on its quantitative easing activities. It shouldn't be news to any investor or individual who reads the paper that interest rates have rapidly moved lower since 2007 and have remained stubbornly low since. When many financial institutions closed their doors or were on the cusp of doing so, the flight-to-quality bid took hold, as investors, governmental entities, and central banks stepped up purchases, sending yields spiraling down. Risk was prevalent in the marketplace. Debt was trading at various prices, representing the risk attached to each name. Some of these prices were an accurate representation of the level of risk that was circulating. This risk was acceptable to certain investors who found the levels to be attractive for the amount of risk at hand. Other investors, however, might not have felt the same way, requiring the bonds to cheapen up even further to gain comfort in the risk-reward trade-off. The two sides waging war on each other had an impact that created the strong move down.

This move down complicates the income stream that is made available to the investor in an income-oriented strategy. As bonds rally, yields move lower and prices increase. The increase in price creates a premium, the amount above the par price. We know that the premium is the equalizer, as it equates newly issued bond yields with the yields of outstanding debt. It doesn't necessarily impact the income generated from the coupons, as long as the new debt introduced to the portfolio carries a similar coupon as the maturing bonds. What is affected is the amount of income that can be withdrawn from the portfolio without reducing the principal amount. This is a battle the market is winning. Investors truly have two primary choices. One is to change the current style of living until interest rates rise, reducing the premiums. This is a hard discussion to have and is a choice that usually doesn't go over too well. The other option is to tap into the principal component of their portfolio to sustain the current level of income. This is a different type of difficult discussion to have, because this option reduces the overall assets or net worth that might be earmarked for gifting in the upcoming years.

In the end, risk is measured and defined by different investors in many different ways. It is important to develop the necessary parameters around how you define and measure risk. Once these parameters are developed, you will have the tools in place to make an educated decision on how to position the portfolio so it is aligned with the overall goals. Through the life of the portfolio, there should be an ongoing analysis that takes place around these metrics, continuing to work them into your portfolio.

RISK-AVERSE INVESTOR

Different investors define risk in different ways. Intuitively, a risk-averse investor is someone who is looking to minimize his or her losses, whether unrealized or realized. In my experience, it is more likely that the investor does not want any losses, whether they are minimal or significant. Whether it is an unrealized or a realized loss, it doesn't matter: It is a loss. Losses are generated for a variety of different reasons. An unrealized loss may result from something as simple as a rise in interest rates. Not to be too simplistic, but it is just a paper loss. You have not crystalized the loss. If the security that you are holding moves higher again in price, your portfolio will again be back in the money. Broadly speaking, as interest rates rise and an unrealized loss is witnessed in the portfolio at some point in time, the move that created this unrealized loss will reverse itself. Bond prices will rise and fall; that is the nature of the market. If the price doesn't rise from investor demand, the price will move back to par as the bond nears maturity; that is the beauty of the bond market.

To fully appreciate the different types of risk that may impact a risk-averse investor, you must look at it on multiple levels. Risk can be broken down into different characteristics. In addition to the fear of losing money, volatility is another characteristic that a risk-averse investor would not want to introduce into his or her portfolio. Volatility is the variation from the average or mean. This is tricky, because volatility can be measured in many different ways. It can be measured through price fluctuation of individual stocks or bonds, portfolio fluctuation, or a combination of both. Volatility can be introduced into the portfolio in many different ways as well, and at times, closely trends with a portfolio's unrealized losses. Figure 5.1 shows the relationship between the 10-year Treasury and the Merrill Lynch Option Volatility Estimate (MOVE) index.

Over the past six years, Treasury securities have had an inherent bid within the market. Whenever there is a spike in volatility represented by the MOVE index, Treasuries have made a sharp move—in this case, rally. Caution is warranted in the sense that the overall surroundings need to be examined. The volatility index will provide the trends to help assess the likelihood of a move, but it will not provide a directional heading. Supply and demand characteristics within the marketplace have a hand in increasing trading, which leads to increased volatility. Amplifying this activity is a very common notion of more buyers than sellers. When that happens, the result is a rallying market. The opposite, more sellers than buyers, will move the market in the other direction. Either way, there is an imbalance that creates excessive movement within your portfolio. Volatility could also be introduced through headline risk. Positive or negative headlines can create

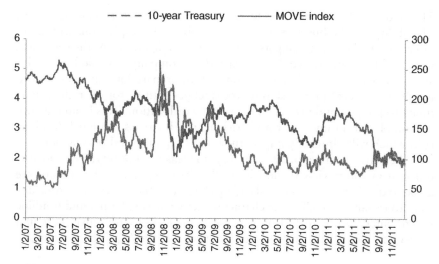

FIGURE 5.1 Treasuries continue to rally as complacency sets in
Source: Bloomberg data and Merrill Lynch MOVE index.

mayhem within a portfolio. Negative headlines are the type to be concerned about. The news may be on a global scale or company specific about an individual security within your portfolio, or even one of their peers.

A PROBLEMATIC TRADE?

On April 20, 2010, a deep-water oil rig run on behalf of British Petroleum (BP) exploded, dumping thousands of barrels of oil into the ocean. It was a nightmare and an unfortunate disaster. As a result, the equity price plunged and bond yields soared. The initial move lower was minimal. As the days and weeks went by with more and more oil entering the Gulf, the situation grew increasingly intense. The impact, which was initially minimal, escalated, seeming at times to be out of control. As the move lower accelerated, investors became more and more jittery. One concern was how to quantify government intervention. Quantifying any government interaction is difficult, if not almost impossible, to do. Was the government going to ban them from drilling off American shores? Was the government going to restrict them some other way? What amount of a fine was the government going to impose? At the time of the event, none of these questions had a straightforward answer, but one thing was certain: additional risk had been introduced into the security's name. To a risk-averse investor, this was problematic.

This action had the potential to result in multiple unfortunate scenarios. The ability for the business to be as profitable was in question, with additional questions surrounding its debt-servicing obligations. At the very least, negative headlines printed daily impacted the company. I would look at this as an exogenous event that is very difficult to prepare for. An investor who is willing to accept more risk is on the sidelines waiting for the right opportunity to jump in and take advantage of the dislocation. This bond may not be suitable for an investor who is risk averse. It carries too much headline risk, which will ultimately impact the bond's liquidity and price action.

There are a number of different ways to measure volatility, risk, and how different investors view them. Ultimately, the end goals of the investor are going to drive how he or she will end up classified. Risk-averse investors may want to refrain from allowing characteristics such as volatility and headline risk to enter into their portfolio. These characteristics are unwelcome in a strategy that is striving for consistent returns and stable principal balance.

RISK-TAKING INVESTOR

Similar to a risk-averse investor, a risk-taking investor can be defined in many different ways. Just as risk comes in many different varieties for a risk-averse investor, an investor who is more comfortable with risk faces it in varying degrees as well. For those investors or accounts that consider themselves at the upper end of the risk spectrum, there are still a few questions to answer. How much risk are you truly talking about? Even the wealthiest investors have a limit to the amount of risk they are willing to take. A loss is a loss, no matter what percentage of the portfolio it represents. If you want to think about it in dollar terms, what is the dollar amount you are unwilling to forgo? To some it may be $100, others, $1,000, or even $100,000 for some. Everyone has a limit and it needs to be identified. What is your comfort level? Here are three areas I like to look at to define the amount of risk you are willing to take:

1. Diversification
     A simple rule of thumb for well-diversified portfolios is to have each position between 0.5 percent and 5 percent. As with any rule, there are exceptions. For a fixed income portfolio that holds government securities such as Treasury notes, it is common to own a larger percentage.

2. Time horizon
     The longer the time period for investment, the higher the likelihood of willingness to take on more risk. For example, an investor whose strategy has a time horizon of 10 years will be willing to take on more

risk than an investor whose strategy has a 2-year duration. If the unfortunate happens and underperformance or losses are generated, there is more time to recoup. These losses could be unrealized or realized.

3. The dreaded dollar loss

Another way to establish a comfort level is to determine how much money the investor is willing to lose from the account. Similar to gambling (I am not saying that investing is the same as gambling), you should gamble with the amount of money that you are willing to lose. The more risk that is introduced into a portfolio, the more comfortable and accepting the end client should be about the possibility of a loss.

Investment risk is not created equally. An investor's comfort level must be met, and it doesn't matter in reaching it if there is minimal or significant risk within. Some feel that with a larger portfolio you are able to risk more money. This may be true; however, if you follow the first rule of thumb and base your investments on a percentage weight, risks are controlled, and it doesn't matter if your portfolio is $50 thousand or $50 million.

DEFINE YOUR STRATEGY

Choices, choices, choices! There are more choices within the investment universe than most investors probably wish to choose from, or need for that matter. I am sure you have heard the statement that you need to work with what you have. That is easier said than done within the fixed income world. What I mean is that we live in a fixed income era in which you have the ability to create a customized portfolio to fit the specific investment needs. The possibilities are limitless. If you are creative and have the ability to look far enough into the future to determine the ultimate goal, the portfolio strategy is a blank slate just waiting for you to start designing. Of course, you need to have an asset manager, if not yourself, who is willing to accommodate your requests. Speaking from experience, there is usually a high probability that most requests will be considered, and if it makes sense from a market perspective, these requests will usually be granted and implemented. What I mean by a market perspective is that there needs to be enough supply in the space you are looking to invest in. There needs to be supply with the right maturities to fund the strategy. Take, for instance, an investor who wants a municipal short-term strategy managed focusing on debt that is issued in Alabama. For this example, short-term may refer to a one-year, three-year, or something in between. The manager, if he or she doesn't know the answer already, should check on the amount of supply that Alabama brings. If there is enough supply, is the supply within the stipulated guidelines, say, the

1- to 3-year bucket? This is very important; I have had requests similar to this one when there is plenty of supply, but all of it is in the 10-year space. That doesn't help when trying to fund and manage a short-term strategy.

Once the broad strategy is decided on, there is another equally-important decision to be made: whether to take an active or a passive approach. This decision should be made prior to the implementation process. There are significant differences between the two strategies. Each strategy carries different benefits that are impactful to a portfolio. There is a defined line that is drawn in the sand separating the portfolios, and ultimately, the management style. Similar to every debate, on one side there are individuals who feel that passive strategies are the best thing since sliced bread, and of course, another side who feels that active management is the best implementation choice. There are pros and cons to both, and along with that, there is not one right or wrong choice. The strategy choice is driven by the risk tolerance, portfolio characteristics, and ultimate goals. One is not better than the other. I do feel that different strategy styles may perform better in different market cycles. Active or passive management styles can be applied to almost any strategy within the fixed income market. There are examples of both of these styles within the mutual fund arena and separate account space. Due to the nature of a separate account, it is easier to construct a portfolio in either style. Let's take a look at the different characteristics that define the different implementations methods. If you take the time to link the commonalities between a passive strategy and a risk-averse investor, it should be very clear that investors with those characteristics may tend to place investments within a passive strategy. It doesn't have to be that way. The likelihood of using a passive strategy as the primary allocation is large. A risk taker may also find success utilizing a passive strategy as a component to the entire portfolio. For example, the addition of a floating-rate note strategy to an active core bond fund may make complete sense. The floating-rate note strategy will help offset the effects of a rising interest environment and the impact to the overall strategy. It is more likely that this type of investor may use a passive element to capture the beta of the market and then take risk where risk should be taken.

There are different names to describe a passive strategy, including low turnover strategy and bond ladder. However it is characterized, a low turnover or passive strategy has a few unique qualities that differentiate it from an active style:

- Lower volatility
- Low turnover
- Limited realized gains and losses
- Consistent income flows

These characteristics are inviting to an investor who may be in a distribution phase of his or her investing life. I say that with caution, though. I have utilized this type of strategy for investors, including myself, who have very specific goals in mind, such as target investing or tax management.

The fixed income markets have gone through events that most portfolio managers and investors wish to forget. A strategy with low volatility and consistent cash flows may sound very enticing. Add the benefit of increased tax management or tax efficiency investing and the package is complete.

ACTIVE STRATEGY

A similar list can be constructed for an active strategy and an investor that classifies as a risk taker. Let's take a look at the characteristics that link a risk taker with an active strategy.

- Increased volatility
- Higher turnover
- Less concern with current income
- Gains and losses are acceptable
- Goal is to beat the benchmark

Active or passive, risk taker or risk-averse investor, the construction of the portfolio is more important than how it is defined. Portfolio construction may take various shapes, but what every strategy shares is the common belief that diversification is ultimately a very important characteristic of any portfolio.

CHAPTER 6

Portfolio Construction

Markets are constantly in a state of uncertainty and flux and money is made by discounting the obvious and betting on the unexpected.

—George Soros

Portfolio construction is a hot discussion topic that always garners attention, and at times, criticism. I wish it were possible to say that there is only one way to construct a portfolio and the directions are as follows. If followed accurately, you would have on your hands a winning portfolio. Unfortunately, as you might have guessed, there is not one single way to construct a portfolio. Whether the portfolio is conservative in nature or more aggressive, there are numerous opinions on the right way to try to reach the end goal. Some methodology is derived from a very technical or formula-heavy approach, while others subscribe to a more fundamental approach. This is then followed up by connecting these goals to the portfolio's strategy.

In this chapter I will walk you through the different aspects of portfolio construction within the fixed income market. I will outline the three factors I deem most important to portfolio construction and the benefit each factor strives to bring to your portfolio over time.

1. Risk defined
2. Aligned goals
3. Portfolio analysis

The order in which these are transacted in is just as important as the factors themselves. As with almost anything in life, portfolio strategy included, it is important to start by defining what you are looking to accomplish before embarking down the path. The three factors are building blocks that, if not followed properly, may not provide a strong foundation. In this case, a solid portfolio may not be attainable.

It is likely that you are familiar with the concept of the efficient frontier. The Markowitz model outlines the concept that provides the greatest return for the amount of risk that the investor is willing to take. Another way to view this is as you increase the amount of risk you take, you improve the potential for an increase in return.[1]

With the recent heightened volatility throughout the global markets and economy, it feels as though the balance between risk and return is skewed or unevenly balanced. What I mean is that there is a visible amount of increased downside risk versus the potential for increased reward. This is prevalent within the financial sector. Uncertainty seems to lie behind every corner and headline. This is most evident at the front end of the market. Risk focused on the points at the front end of the curve has always been there, and that is not going to change. Investors are, however, more recently in tune with this notion as the market volatility has increased, creating havoc in fixed income portfolios. The concept of risk versus return should be utilized within the portfolio, within the various asset classes, and for some investors, at each individual security level. At a minimum, the risk should be reviewed at a high level and at the individual security level, which may include monitoring correlations and spread activity.

FACTOR 1: DEFINING YOUR RISK

Just as we defined different types of end investors and portfolio strategies in the previous chapter, we need to take that information and relate it to the preconstruction stage of building the fixed income portfolio. When deciding on the build of a portfolio, a handful of questions need to be answered. These questions include:

- What is the time frame for my investments?
- Is volatility a concern?
- What is the goal for my investments?

These questions will help you shape your portfolio appropriately. Recent years have proven to be difficult for investors for a number of reasons. If your portfolio is constructed with holes and your goals are not aligned properly to your portfolio, a difficult environment will become that much

---

[1]Bloomberg on efficient frontier Markowitz.

more difficult. For instance, if you are very concerned with volatility, let the equity piece of your portfolio provide the roller-coaster ride. Depending on your risk tolerance, you may not want to introduce added volatility through your fixed income allocation within your portfolio.

FACTOR 2: ALIGNING GOALS

Portfolio construction discussions are usually centered on the allocation between an equity allocation, fixed income, and possibly alternatives. The different allocation or weight between these sectors is usually aligned to the current life stage that the investor may be in. Alignment may also be linked, but not limited, to the portfolio's specific goals. On a cursory level, initial research and common sense tell you that the longer the investment horizon, the more aggressive the investment allocation is likely to be. The reverse occurs as well. In a traditional equity/bond model, the more risk-averse the investor is, the greater the focus on the fixed income allocation. Another way to view this relationship is the closer in reaching the ultimate goal, the greater the fixed income exposure. Simply put, a traditional fixed income asset class is viewed as providing less volatility than the equity markets.

What happens if the portfolio is constructed entirely of fixed income securities? Portfolio goals and strategy should be looked at in similar fashion. Different sectors within the fixed income market carry different characteristics and possible returns. It should not be surprising that over time, the high-yield market (represented by the Bank of America Merrill Lynch U.S. High Yield Master II Constrained index) provides increased returns over the U.S. Treasury sector (represented by the Bank of America Merrill Lynch U.S. Treasury Master index) or even the corporate sector (represented by the Bank of America Merrill Lynch U.S. Corporate Master index), providing greater absolute returns over the Treasury sector. Table 6.1 shows the three sectors discussed. It is clear that the sectors move in and out of favor. This gyration has the potential to make it very difficult to perfectly time a move. Because perfect timing is difficult, there is an increased possibility of falling into the trap of buying high and selling low, in this case rotating in and out of the sector at the most disadvantageous time. There are multiple sectors and subsectors within the fixed income market. I chose the following five sectors represented by an appropriate index for comparison of absolute returns. There is not one sector that predominately outperformed over the time period.

Fixed income sectors are not known to carry high correlations. Table 6.2 shows the correlations to the U.S. Treasury sector. I opted not to run the correlations against all asset classes and just used the Treasury sector as the

TABLE 6.1   Index Returns Show that Diversification Matters

	U.S. Treasury Master Index	U.S. Corporate Master Index	U.S. High Yield Master II Constrained Index
1991	15.20	18.24	
1992	7.21	9.12	
1993	10.63	12.43	
1994	−3.35	−3.34	
1995	18.45	21.55	
1996	2.61	3.39	
1997	9.62	10.39	**12.91**
1998	**10.03**	8.72	2.94
1999	−2.38	−1.89	2.43
2000	**13.37**	9.14	−5.20
2001	6.74	**10.70**	4.48
2002	**11.57**	10.17	−0.53
2003	2.26	8.31	27.97
2004	3.50	5.42	10.87
2005	**2.81**	1.97	2.78
2006	3.14	4.38	10.76
2007	**9.06**	4.64	2.53
2008	**13.98**	−6.82	−26.11
2009	−3.72	19.76	58.10
2010	5.88	9.52	15.07
2011	**9.79**	7.51	4.37

Bold represents highest return.
Source: Bank of America Merrill Lynch Global Index System.

base. The reason for this is straightforward. The U.S. Treasury market is looked at as the plain vanilla triple-A security, carrying little to no credit risk. Historically, I would have said no credit risk, but due to events over the past couple of years, there needs to be at least the consideration of credit risk when speaking to this sector. As an example, the correlation between the Treasury sector and high-yield is −.714; that is almost 100 percent not correlated.

This is just one example in favor of diversification. Remember that in the end, if the goal of the portfolio is to achieve consistent returns over the long run, diversification within various sectors is crucial. Later in this chapter, I will stress the importance of diversification and give a few individual security rules on how to remain well diversified.

TABLE 6.2   Correlation to U.S. Treasury market

Sectors	Treasury
Treasury	1
Agency	0.897
High-Yield	−0.714
Corporate	0.367
MBS	0.868
Time frame:	
TSY/Corp 1999–2011	
TSY/HY 1997–2011	
TSY/USD Agency 2000–2011	
TSY/MBS 1999–2011	

Source: Bank of America Merrill Lynch Global Index System and Bloomberg data.

A sole fixed income portfolio should be addressed the same way as investing within multiple asset classes using portfolio goals or specific characteristics. In addition, aligning a portfolio with particular risk tolerance, possible covenants, and cash flow analysis are used.

This is where I like to restate the back-to-basics theme. There is no denying that a fixed income portfolio has risk, albeit a different type of risk than your equity or alternative asset classes. A fixed income portfolio should not be the asset class where you are taking the majority of your risk. The trade-off is just not there. There are rewards; however, these rewards usually do not compare to those in other asset classes, such as equities, alternatives, or any other higher-beta asset classes.

Take risk where you get paid for taking risk. Figure 6.1 shows a common basic depiction of the trade-off between risk and reward.

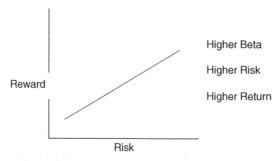

FIGURE 6.1   Trade-off between Risk and Reward

There are different sectors that, at times, are utilized to enhance the portfolio yield or return within the fixed income arena. This may be accomplished through leverage or through higher-beta sectors. In general, when used, an allocation should be minimal. I am not saying to completely abstain from these sectors; just tread lightly. The examples that follow do not include these higher-beta sectors.

Conservative Strategy

The first option all investors have at their disposal is to hide their money under the mattress or in a lockbox in the basement of corporate headquarters. This is the most conservative approach to take, and with money market yields near zero, the mattress may become more appealing. If this option is selected, risks such as fire, theft, and poor sleep due to a lumpy mattress must be mitigated.

Aside from the "bank o' mattress"—which, to be clear, is not really an option—there are varying degrees of conservative strategies. There is always a money market fund, but unfortunately yields are paltry. A more aggressive strategy—the next step or level of risk—is an all-Treasury or government fund. There are positive characteristics with this strategy. To start with, the securities are guaranteed by the U.S. government and carry little to no credit risk. One problem, and potentially a serious one, is that the portfolio is not diversified very well. A secondary concern with this strategy is that it may not keep pace with inflation. It is possible to have a conservative approach while hitting the necessary points to make the portfolio strong and successful. What this strategy won't do is provide you with a government guarantee and a high coupon or yield for the portfolio. Those two characteristics just don't go hand in hand, but they are probably the two most common requests I receive in constructing a portfolio. My answer is always the same. First, I apologize in advance, then I provide the choice to either receive a government guarantee through the Treasury sector or other government products or to receive a more aggressive portfolio attaining a higher yield—just not both at the same time. That is how most of those discussions end.

Let's look at a couple of options. Figure 6.2 shows a starting point with a conservative allocation.

This sector allocation represents a conservative allocation with reflection of portfolio goals.

These samples are the starting point or the beginning of the building blocks. The weights can and should be changed to meet risk tolerance, market conditions, and portfolio goals. In the first example, a money market strategy, an investor would expect to have little to no principal volatility and have his or her money available when needed. From the investor's point of

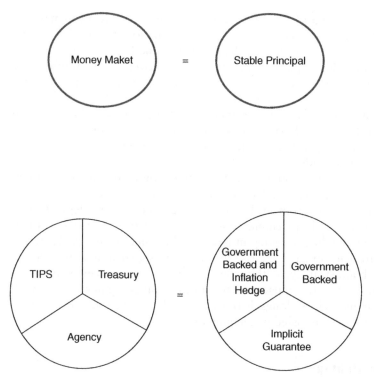

FIGURE 6.2 Money Market Strategy Satisfies a Goal of Stable Principal

view, risk should not be a daily concern. The portfolio manager, on the other hand, should be dissecting and calculating risk on a daily basis, every second of the day. The recent environment created a backdrop where a manager must take nothing for granted. I don't want to say that everything known should be forgotten, but it should be looked at with a new perspective or through a different set of glasses. There are multiple sayings that could be applied here, but the bottom line is that nothing should be taken for granted. At times, the market tests everything that has been learned over a lifetime of investing.

A money market or cash strategy could be implemented in a mutual fund or a separate account. Either way, the focus is (in this order): preservation of capital, liquidity, and yield. There are benefits to each vehicle. I will outline the benefits within the separate account section later in this chapter.

The second example is a step to the more aggressive side. A better way to describe it may be a step away from the most conservative side. The portfolio has the ability to be constructed with debt issued by the U.S. government. The greater the percentage of Treasury securities, the more comfort you may gain in that portfolio strategy. Both the Treasury Inflation-Protected Securities (TIPS) and U.S. Treasuries carry the backing of the U.S. government. The agency sector holds a quasi-guarantee from the government. Another way to look at the agency sector with regards to the guarantee is to say that it has implicit guarantee—an implied backstop from the U.S. government. It is important to note that these sectors are just the building blocks. Actual weights can be changed. Through the steps of portfolio construction you, the portfolio manager, will have the ability to make any necessary changes that would provide additional comfort.

If you have trouble coming to terms with the thought of a loss in principal, then you should again go back to basics and invest in the sectors that are closely tied to the government. Investing in a conservative strategy utilizing government sectors helps eliminate many risks. Interest rate risk is a risk that will remain when investing in most fixed income strategies. There are strategies to help mitigate the rise in interest rates, such as implementing a laddered bond strategy. Within construction of that strategy, you will be able to help control the impact of rising rates by investing in securities with shorter-term maturities alongside those across the yield curve. This strategy and others will be discussed in Chapter 11.

Moderate Strategy

Just as an asset manager would work his or her way out on the risk curve within an equity portfolio, the same should happen within the fixed income markets. Higher-beta slices should be increased while reducing the lower-beta sleeves. One way to accomplish this is to reduce your government exposure. As the portfolio increases the overall risk, it makes more sense to diagram the asset class versus goal. Figure 6.3 shows one example of how a portfolio can move out along the risk curve by introducing additional sectors. The introduction of high yield and a core bond fund represented by the Barclays Capital Aggregate index would create a more aggressive strategy. The actual weights will vary depending on risk tolerance and profile.

More Aggressive Strategy

Taking the strategy up another notch in the risk metrics can be accomplished in many ways. Simply changing exposure to the current asset classes will provide opportunity to achieve increased yield and/or return. For example, Figure 6.4 compares the moderate strategy with an aggressive model. It is clear that a more aggressive strategy may be created using the same sectors

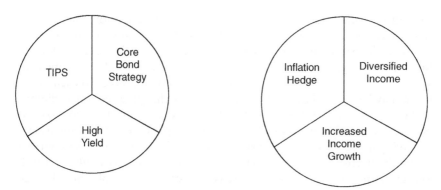

FIGURE 6.3 Moderate sector allocation with portfolio goals

as the moderate strategy, with greater emphasis on the high yield and less with the TIPS strategy.

We know that these are not the only asset classes in the fixed income market. Keeping it straightforward and clean is important for providing an example, which is why I limited the example to these sectors. Asset-backed securities and mortgage securities are two other asset classes that are usually utilized when investing within the fixed income markets. Both these sectors received a bad reputation and were dragged down through the mud in 2008 and 2009 when both the fixed income and equity markets were imploding. As with any security, there are securities within these asset classes that carry a greater degree of risk than others. If the proper homework is done on all the underlying securities that create the asset-backed security or MBS, you

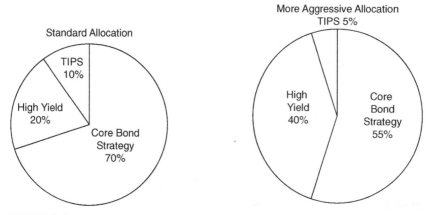

FIGURE 6.4 Typical sector allocation compared to a more aggressive allocation

can find securities that offer value. After meticulous attention and analysis, these sectors have the ability to add additional diversification to the portfolio as well as the potential for increased return. These securities are much more difficult to analyze and at times purchase than the typical government or corporate bond. There is a greater number of moving pieces to each bond, which may be affected by a shifting market or a changing economic climate.

A word of caution: Most core bond strategies have an allocation to these sectors. Because they have an allocation, it is imperative to know the weight if weaving in this strategy with a slice of the specific sector. This is important so that the portfolio isn't unknowingly overexposed to a particular sector. If your target for asset-backed exposure is 5 percent, it is simple enough to go out to the market and add that exposure to your portfolio. However, if the core bond strategy or allocation already has holdings within this sector of 4 percent, in reality your overall exposure is greater than the target weight. Figure 6.5 shows how an aggressive model or strategy snapshot may look.

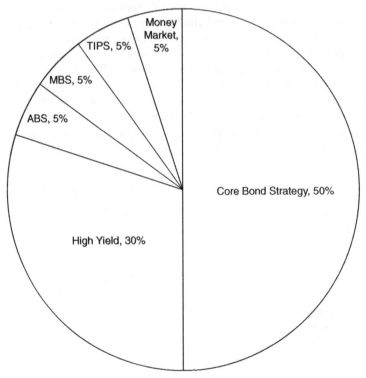

FIGURE 6.5   Representation of what a more aggressive allocation may look like

The allocation and alignment of strategy is driven from the end client's profile. The strategy is sometimes dictated by other factors; however, whatever the methodology is, it is important to remain disciplined to the strategy that encompasses the necessary goals. It is also worth noting that it is possible to measure risk through various statistical models. There may be a more efficient way to allocate the sectors discussed in Figure 6.4 while achieving a similar expected return. The chosen allocation is to start the discussion and build an efficient risk-adjusted model.

FACTOR 3: PORTFOLIO ANALYSIS

It almost sounds counterintuitive to recommend analyzing a portfolio prior to investing in a new strategy or amending a current strategy. Determining whether it does or doesn't, is the third step to portfolio construction. This is a very crucial step. It is paramount that the portfolio be in alignment with the investor's or investment policy statement's goals. Transitioned portfolios may hold securities that at one time fit the investor's current strategy but are not aligned anymore. Another challenge is that the investment environment is ever-changing and the current environment may not be as favorable for the specific holdings within the portfolio. That is not to say that the same holdings were not in favor at one time.

In a perfect world, a portfolio set for construction would hold only a cash position. Although possible, it is not likely, unless an existing portfolio was liquidated, or perhaps the investor received a windfall of money. I have to admit, anytime I receive a portfolio to manage that is holding a sole cash position, a smile comes to my face. Understandably, in an all-cash transition, there is no need to worry about earmarking which securities to liquidate and which to keep in the portfolio.

The reality is, an investment portfolio usually holds a handful of securities. These are legacy securities and frequently have a story or some history to them. For that reason alone, all factors need to be discussed and flushed out prior to analysis so that the manager knows what he or she truly has to work with. The portfolio may hold a bond that is so far out of the money or in the money that the end investor is not willing to sell because the activity will create additional tax complications. There are also incidents when an investor receives a recommendation from someone of influence or significance and the relationship between the individuals is stronger than the outcome of the security. I am not sure if I would agree with that view, but this information is needed when assessing the portfolio.

When reviewing an existing portfolio there needs to be a similar, if not identical, process that occurs when allocating cash to fund a strategy. A replicable process provides strong and consistent results.

A game plan needs to be utilized when the initial review takes place. Make no mistake that if a process does not exist, one should be created. What I found best and very simple to construct is a document with the pertinent information that is necessary to conduct your analysis, and ultimately a conclusion to either sell or hold an existing portfolio. Notice I didn't say add to a current position. Adding to a position, and there are some exceptions, is at times very difficult to achieve. Supply within the fixed income world is quite different from the world of equities. It is very easy to add exposure of a particular company within the equity space. You go out to the exchange and purchase the shares you are looking to acquire. That luxury doesn't exist in the fixed income world. This holds true specifically within the municipal sector and credit markets. The reason this occurs is that once debt is issued and taken down by investors, there may not be another chance to purchase that specific bond again unless the issuer reopens the deal. What this means is that it may be very difficult to add to existing positions, and that every portfolio may not look identical to one another.

The piece that I am describing above should contain enough information to provide you with comfort. I have always used a variety of different characteristics for review. I don't feel that there should be a set number required to paint a clear picture. The characteristics should be customized, covering the necessary information needed for your analysis to be effective. Different sectors will carry different categories for analysis. For instance, the mortgage sector will require different areas to analyze than the agency or corporate sector.

I feel the following 10 categories provide the necessary information to start your analysis:

1. Issuer name
2. CUSIP
3. Years to maturity
4. Duration
5. Agency ratings
6. Coupon
7. Yield information
8. Credit view
9. Position weight
10. Embedded optionality

These data points were chosen because they paint a picture of the security that leads to a recommendation. The basics, such as duration and yields, are noted, as is an opinion on the credit itself. The opinion could be twofold. First, there is a summary from the rating agency on the credit. In addition, and more importantly, there is the view and analysis from the credit team. A credit opinion could resemble the following example, which is for a municipal health care bond:

- The health care sector may come under additional pressure due to proposed legislation.
- There is increased volatility within the issuer as there are signs of softening within funding.
- There is exposure to a significant amount of derivatives.
- Balance sheet is highly levered.

These are just some examples of characteristics that would help shape the view of a particular credit. The third bullet would stand out in particular with me. Because this is a municipal issuer, a health care or hospital bond, I get worried when there is a significant amount of derivative exposure. That is a definite red flag. I would not want to own debt, municipal or taxable, that has any type of indirect exposure within their business that wasn't part of the core business model or the normal course of business. That model is just asking for trouble. Following the summary of data points, a recommendation is made whether to hold or sell the security. Everything discussed thus far is looked at from a fundamental approach. When debt is reviewed, it normally has a binary outcome—you either like it or you don't. At times, there are grey areas that complicate matters. It shouldn't be a surprise that complications come with the territory.

There are other factors that influence the decision to hold or to sell existing debt. From a fundamental perspective, if the credit opinion is negative, the decision is easy and straightforward: sell the debt. It is common that debt in an existing portfolio does not fit the new investment strategy. If anything is straightforward, this concept is. All bonds that are to be held in the portfolio must fit the new investment strategy and guidelines. Strategy guidelines that state all bonds must have a final stated maturity no longer than ten years are easy to understand. Any bond that has a final stated maturity longer than ten years should automatically be rejected. A bond holding a final stated maturity of twenty years should never make it into the portfolio. The same would hold true for a bond that doesn't meet other criteria such as credit quality.

Diversification needs to be assessed as well at this point. If you have listened to me present on this topic or spoken to me directly this example should resonate with you. It is difficult to begin to try to quantify how many times poor diversification occurs. It happens time and time again, and once you think the environment has changed, it becomes clear that it really hasn't changed at all. That is the search for yield. I am not referring to the search for yield through the typical diversification within a strategy. What I am about to describe is looking at an offering sheet, sorting it from highest yield to lowest, and picking the top ten bonds. These bonds are picked on what seems to be only yield, neglecting fundamentals or other characteristics.

Once again, I will refer to the fall of 2008. It was very common to see accounts with minimal holdings and a very highly concentrated sector. The most outrageous example that came across my desk was a portfolio with only six holdings, all within the financial sector. To make matters worse, those six holdings all in the financial sector comprised just a few names, specifically the four large investment banks that, unfortunately, were in the daily headlines. The noise around these banks set the backdrop and the landscape for higher yields. It seems that these yields are what drove the investment decision. Whoever constructed this portfolio was seeking out yield and only yield. The risk-reward trade off was overlooked. As the market imploded, the common scenario unfolded. The portfolio value decreased rapidly because it was not well diversified across many measures.

Reduction of Credit Risk

If you are looking for consistent long-term results, once again, there needs to be a focus around a disciplined investment approach. Through this approach risk will be mitigated. Diversification is a key contributor within the process to reduce risk. The essentials within portfolio construction focus around a credit review approach that provides the groundwork for proper diversification. When success is found through diversification, you will realize a sense of control. In a nutshell, diversification is looked at by some at the security level. That is an accurate assessment, although lacking. Diversification should be taken a few steps further. A solid philosophy for diversification and portfolio construction encompasses not only credit-specific, but sector and regional analysis driving diversification. Diversification should encompass multiple levels and can be accomplished through five categories:

1. Product diversification
2. Issuer diversification
3. Sector diversification
4. Geographic diversification
5. Quality diversification

This approach thoroughly covers multiple fronts on diversification. This multilayer approach will help provide success within the portfolio toward the generation of consistent results. Relate this view back to the example of the investment banks that were held in a portfolio. All five of the diversification measures were not met. All securities were fixed-rate corporate notes; therefore, product diversification was not met. The fact that there were only six bonds and all were financial institutions from the U.S. negates issuer, sector, and geographic diversification rules. Finally, the quality measure may be interpreted different ways. I look at both the actual rating of the security and where it stands within the capital structure. Depending on the timing, this measure may have been adhered to at the time of purchase. There is the possibility that it was not, particularly if the positions were acquired in or around the time of the financial crisis when the entire sector was under attack from rating agencies with downgrades.

Outlined next is a representation of diversification and limits. The first section represents the taxable market, followed by an example from the municipal sector.

These position limits may be viewed either as soft limits or hard and fast rules. I subscribe to the notion of implementing them as a soft rule, with a hard rule slightly above. What I mean is that a 3 percent single-A limit is a soft rule; however, if due to market value swings or cash flows, the position creeps up to 4 percent, the hard rule would be to reduce the position by at least 1 percent. The move higher would trigger action, which may be to pare back exposure or, depending on the circumstances, hold firm.

Securities represented within the corporate sector should have a rating from at least one nationally recognized rating agency, if not two. This is driven by the internal credit review process. If the credit process is strong, one rating may be sufficient. The individual security limits should be thought of and structured in a tiered fashion. For instance, a triple-A security, the highest possible credit rating, would have a 7 percent allowable maximum limit. This weight is established at the time of purchase. The limit needs to be calculated at the issuer level. That is, the individual issues must be rolled up to the parent company. A company's finance arm needs to be looked at just as the parent is, as well any commercial paper that is issued by the company. It doesn't stop with commercial paper. Any security that is backed or supported by the parent needs to be counted as well.

As you work your way down the credit curve, the weight of each position is reduced. An example would be for double-A to have an allowable 3 to 5 percent weight; single-A, 1 to 2 percent; and triple-B, 0.5 to 1 percent.

Government Securities

A similar concept should be utilized when allocating government securities. It is slightly different, because these securities are associated with the government and have the backstop and pockets of the same entity. Individual U.S. Treasury securities have no limit at the security level. Best judgment should be used to avoid curve risk through too much exposure in one issue and point on the curve. Explicit government guaranteed corporate debt may have a 10 percent allowable limit. If you remember, this is the debt that was issued back in 2008 and 2009 when the market was imploding and liquidity was scarce. In some cases, corporate issuers would not have been able to issue debt and receive funding without the help of the U.S. government. Since the downturn, corporate issuance with government backing has been nonexistent. This is to be expected moving forward, unless there is another global disruption where the government needs to step in. Hopefully the likelihood of that occurring is minimal.

Agency securities that carry the implicit guarantee by the government could be held to 5 to 10 percent per issue unless otherwise stated in the investment policy statement or portfolio guideline.

When it comes to setting limits for sub debt, the equation becomes a little more difficult. Some individuals group the sub debt in under the agency guidelines. I feel more comfortable adhering to the credit guidelines. One reason for the disparity is because sub debt does not have the same type of liquidity as senior debt. Also, if push comes to shove, there is the possibility that the government may decide to lift the implicit guarantee from the sub debt while continuing to support the senior debt. If this were to happen, the market would not look favorably on this activity.

Similar criteria and actions should be upheld within the municipal market as well. Again, these position limits may be viewed as soft limits or hard rule. The municipal sector is inherently less liquid. As a result, careful consideration needs to be taken when assessing any actions that may occur due to a downgrade. Due to the nature of the sector, specifically within a separate account structure, I would hold true to the percentage owned at the time of purchase.

There are two different times these percentages could be calculated for qualification. I find that the when implementing diversification requirements, they act as a reflection and help paint an accurate picture when they are calculated at the time of purchase. Some professionals may use the weight at the time of purchase, converting this methodology to market value subsequent to the purchase. The combination of the two, including a tiered approach as described earlier, works the best. If the diversification limits are breached, this does not mean that an automatic sell is required. If the percentage increases due to cash flows, it should be at the discretion of the management team to decide whether to reduce the position or continue to hold. Cash flows are sometimes replenished quickly, resulting automatically in the reduction of the percentage owned. Each portfolio is likely different and only the history of the account will provide guidance. Usually, flows within a mutual fund are replenished at a quicker pace than in a separate account, because there are multiple investors within the product rather than a single investor in a separate account.

Once a security is purchased, what is the process to follow if a downgrade happens? It is unrealistic to think that a downgrade will not happen. In recent years, with the volatile environment we have lived and invested through, downgrades seem to occur more frequently and with greater magnitude. The simple one-notch downgrade at times seems like a thing of the past. Two- and three-notch downgrades, and sometimes even more, feel as if they occur on a more frequent basis than ever before.

In the event of a downgrade, a formal review from the credit analyst covering the issuer and portfolio manager should commence. The analysis should start within 24 to 48 hours, with a formal decision and documentation within a reasonable time frame. A logical time frame may be determined by current market conditions and the degree of the downgrade. The findings should determine if any action needs to be taken due to change in the outright credit quality or specific portfolio guidelines.

The idea is that by adhering to the aforementioned weights prior to any purchases and frequently monitoring positions, the portfolio will automatically maintain a balance and remain well diversified. The positions should be reviewed daily by the portfolio manager, and formally at a weekly investment policy committee meeting. These two actions will help reduce volatility and mitigate overall risk.

The recipe for a solidly constructed portfolio is to efficiently and successfully piece together securities that hold characteristics that are allowable within the portfolio's guidelines. These credits need to be filtered minding the five levels of diversification. Once filtered, they next need to be most advantageously utilized in a way that constructs a solid portfolio. The strength of the portfolio will help mitigate risk while providing the necessary characteristics to effectively reach all stipulated goals.

Risks to Consider

Throughout the course of investing, you will no doubt encounter different interest rate environments. No matter what the environment is, the current rate environment should help shape the portfolio you are constructing.

Interest Rate Environment   Interest rates are always shifting, many times driven by investor demand and the economic landscape. The rise and fall of interest rates doesn't necessarily stop there. Many times an exogenous event occurs, changing investor sentiment and possibly long-term outlooks, which will impact the environment. The yield curve can shift and twist in parallel fashion either up or down, or flatten or steepen. Whichever path is taken, the effects on a portfolio may be drastically different. As explained earlier, this is why, within the construction phase, the current and expectation for future interest rates must be taken into consideration.

I am not going to spend a lot of time describing a falling interest rate environment. As interest rates fall, prices rise, usually benefiting the portfolio. A rising interest rate environment, normally associated with a bear market, is much more challenging to navigate through.

A rising rate environment has the ability to play havoc with a fixed income portfolio. There are ways to combat this move. Let's be real here for a moment. If interest rates rise, almost any fixed income portfolio will be negatively impacted in some way. By introducing different asset classes, the manager has the ability to mitigate the risks.

Floating Rate Notes   Adding floating rate note securities is one way to tie the portfolio to different indexes that move with interest rates. Floaters are issued in a variety of asset classes from corporate securities to agency debt. The U.S. Treasury is even considering the possible launch of a floating rate Treasury note. The addition of a floating rate note will benefit the portfolio predominantly in an environment where short-term rates are moving higher. If the yield curve steepens where the long end moves higher with little to no effect on the front end, floating rate notes may still outperform longer-dated bonds; however, the coupons tied to these notes will not be adjusted.

My belief is that a separate account is the optimal vehicle to use in a bear market or rising interest rate environment. There are different opinions around this topic with some probably strongly disagreeing with my view. There are benefits as well as drawbacks to a separate account. In the end, the deciding factor will be driven by the investment goals.

A mutual fund is the common alternative to a separate account. The primary difference between a separate account and a mutual fund is the number of investors within each vehicle. A separate account is unique to the owner of the account. This singular ownership provides different benefits to the investor, institutional or otherwise. What that means is that the investor has full transparency into the account. They are able to see each individual holding. These holdings that are used to complete the strategy are also customized to the investor's goals. Due to the nature of the account, if the investor's goals change over time, it is fairly simple to adjust or realign the objective of the strategy to their goals. This is the customization feature that coincides with a separate account. Lastly, your assets are yours and are only affected by the actions you take. The securities you are invested in are not subject to other investor's activity. For example, if a group of investors are becoming jittery and start to redeem their shares from the mutual fund, there is a chance that the fund managers may need to liquidate or raise cash at unopportunistic times. That type of activity may negatively affect the fund, as the net asset value (NAV) may drop, lowering the value of your holding. In a separate account, the only assets that are held are your assets. If you want to liquidate you may, but more importantly, if you want to hold firm to your positions and ride out the volatility, that is your choice and is easily accomplished.

In addition to a rising rate environment, there are other risks that need to be considered in fixed income portfolio construction:

- Lack of liquidity or a frozen market
- An inflationary environment
- Credit risk

A market characterized by little liquidity, or even frozen, is a nightmare for managers to navigate. It has happened time and time again, particularly when a crisis—or what is perceived to be a crisis—materializes. It is possible to track back to almost any major correction and watch how quickly liquidity evaporates from the system. The occurrence could be driven by instances at a macro level or caused by a systemic event, but there are also times when an event is centered on just one security or a particular sector—more of an idiosyncratic risk. Impact on one security, if that was to happen, may initially be minimal at the portfolio level. If the occurrences grow and the ripple effect takes hold, it might become more problematic.

Think about what happens if the singular event starts to snowball. The snowball effect moves from the initial company to others in the sector. What if there is fear that those names in the sector will negatively impact other names in a completely different sector? There are a lot of what-ifs involved in this example. Unfortunately, that is the way these situations develop and need to be looked at. A single instance can easily develop into a larger problem that will affect the liquidity of the portfolio. The absence of liquidity will drive prices lower, if you are lucky enough to receive a price at all.

Inflation Inflation is damaging to a fixed income portfolio, just as it is to the consumer. Inflation erodes the dollar and the markets. If your dollar is worth less tomorrow than it is today, you will be unhappy. The same concept applies to fixed income securities. The value of a bond held today does not hold the same value tomorrow if inflation is running higher. If the inflation rate is moving higher, interest rates are going to follow the same path. As interest rates move up, bond prices move down, and your portfolio becomes worth less. A different way to look at this is that a bond with a 2 percent coupon is not going to be as attractive to someone if inflation is present; the 2 percent coupon you are receiving is not going to have the same purchasing power now as it did when inflation was nonexistent. The investor is now going to demand a higher coupon and yield if inflation is picking up and eroding his investment.

Credit Risk   Credit risk is probably one of the most straightforward risks the bond market faces. Although it is straightforward at times, it may be masked by other elements within the market. Investors grasping for hope and speculation are sometimes the biggest culprits behind present or hidden credit risk. Credit risks may materialize from either fundamental or event-driven characteristics. Fundamental risk, I believe, is easier to uncover than technical risk. Balance sheet analysis together with earnings calls usually provides enough information to develop a solid view and opinion. As with anything, the goal is to spot an early-developing trend. In a perfect world, the trend would be uncovered in its infancy stage so you have ample time to take action if needed. For example, take the pharmaceutical sector. If a company's pipeline is slowing and a prominent drug is coming off patent (meaning generics will be developed and soon be competing) there is a pretty good chance that earnings may start to slow or at least show signs of slowing. The slowdown in earnings may drive the company to start or increase the burn rate of its available cash, applying more toward research and development or even a possible acquisition with the hopes of building a new pipeline through acquisition.

In some instances, activity happens at a rapid pace, too fast for fundamentals to provide a downward or even a sideways trend. Unfortunately, there is a lag between an event and the materialization of facts laying the groundwork for the fundamentals to develop. Too common an example is when a company has an accident that will immediately impact its earnings and ultimately its cash on hand. Oil spills or automotive recalls certainly fall into this category. Instantaneously when the headline is reported over the tape or news wire, the company's outstanding debt begins to be repriced. There is usually an initial gap lower while investors analyze the headlines and use their best judgment to calculate what price they feel the bond should trade at. A different approach to get to the same answer is to attempt to calculate what price the company is worth after the accident. Assumptions will need to be made on different outcomes. Always remember to include the high-probability and low-probability events. It doesn't hurt to prepare for the worst-case scenario, even if it the odds of it materializing are very low. Because additional credit risk is created from an unfortunate event, it may at times seem very difficult or nearly impossible to accurately calculate and make a decision as the data are just being reported. You are not cutting diamonds; you just need to be in the ballpark.

As with anything, there are varying degrees of risk depending on the security. Risk takes on many shapes and varieties, and when constructing a portfolio they all need to be calculated. Daily investors wrestle with minimal risk that usually only impacts the price of the security and should be viewed as temporary. From time to time, events arise that create substantial risk to a company, bringing into question the company's ability to remain a going concern. In the end, whether you are uncovering minimal risk or substantial risk, what it really comes down to is that one question: Is the company solvent or not?

BOTTOM LINE

In an environment that poses multiple challenges, fixed income investing needs to be examined differently than in previous years. Asset managers are not only responsible for generating alpha; they must also take an active approach to bring risks down. These two goals do go hand in hand, though the reduction of risk is at times overlooked.

In an environment that is conducive to investing, there is never much question about risk or positioning. When the markets are good, everyone is usually happy and questions are kept to a minimum. Unfortunately, this can change on a dime. Risk and positioning are two concepts that always rear their ugly heads when markets are stressed. Think about how many more questions arise or the number of times a portfolio is analyzed when the markets are moving lower. A global disruption or a disruption that materializes on local soil creates a similar effect. At any point when either of these circumstance or others similar in nature arise, the first thought that should cross your mind is to reduce risk. When these circumstances materialize, the rule of thumb is to reduce the size of your bets. As you reduce the bets, the overall risk to a fixed income portfolio should naturally decline.

Make no mistake—outpacing markets is difficult to do on a consistent basis. The low interest rate environment that has impacted everyone has created an even more difficult environment to construct a portfolio. New headaches were created as financial institutions needed additional capital to survive. Unfortunately, there is not a quick cure on the horizon. Investors need to prepare themselves and their portfolios to accommodate the new environment. The bottom line is that you need to construct a strategy to fit your needs and weather the events that the market and economy may throw your way.

CHAPTER 7

Asset Allocation

In the business world, the rearview mirror is always clearer than the windshield.

—Warren Buffett

Asset allocation is an integral piece of investing. This chapter will discuss the broad theme of asset allocation and why it is necessary. I will walk you through laying the groundwork for tracking the markets and applying what you see to your strategy, and show the specific need for going global. A more detailed outline of creating an asset allocation mix was covered in Chapter 6, Portfolio Construction.

Image you are driving across the country and you come to a fork in the road. This fork is unique. Instead of the typical fork with three or four prongs, you are faced with a six-pronged fork yielding multiple decisions to make. This a daunting task, to say the least, that all investors at one time or another have encountered. Adding uncertainty to the mix is the fact that not one of the prongs is labeled. There is no information showing up on your car's GPS system, and even your map is blank. All you have to go on is your instinct. Unfortunately, your instinct doesn't go too far, and may fall short even when it comes to providing comfort to the passengers in your car.

Now picture each prong of that fork as a different segment of the fixed income market. From an investment perspective, markets rarely telegraph a direct route or paint a clear picture of future movements. This opaqueness can leave investors disorientated and less than 100 percent confident in the current and future state of the economy and markets. If you have ever been in that state, you know how it feels, and it is not pleasant. Looking through clouded glasses is not a position that anyone wants to find themselves in when there is money on the line.

Markets do, however, provide data points. It is these data points that need to be embraced and utilized to provide direction. These points are to be used as a guide. While some of the best investors have incredible instincts, proper tools still aid in the decision-making process. These tools are used to capture the turning points, reversals, and momentum shifts that may impact the fixed income strategies. To capture the different indicators, you need a starting point. Just as a map is needed at the fork in the road, a map needs to be developed to help navigate through the ins and outs of the market and economy, providing to you and any passengers that are picked up along the way a path to success.

THE ROAD MAP

Markets today are tightly intertwined, which can make them that much more difficult to dissect. If you had a time machine to take you back a decade or two, the interaction between markets would look very different. As with anything, markets evolve. New products are engineered to create wealth and to protect the wealth that has already been created. At first glance, the launch of any new securities sets the expectation of increased efficiencies. Efficiencies are then followed by added transparency, and in the world of investing that means everything.

Transparency is much sought after today as global markets are converging. Once, what seems like many years ago, sectors were not viewed as one functioning entity. The notion of being intertwined to the extent that markets and sectors are today didn't exist. Even prior to the financial crisis that surfaced in 2007, the markets were separated in what I refer to as silos. Each sector or asset class had its own unique silo. Information was not crossbred or transferred frequently from a manger within one asset class to one in another. At the time, it didn't seem as necessary as it does today. Asset managers who ran money market funds were focused primarily on securities within the money market arena, as were portfolio managers within other asset classes as well. I am not saying that they didn't follow other sectors or express views about the economy. They did, and I am speaking from experience here—when I ran a money market mutual fund, we tracked and followed numerous indicators and followed different sectors. The difference is that today, what is happening on the mortgage or swap desk is more closely watched and analyzed with the goal of pinpointing any, if not all, possible risks and outcomes if there were a meltdown or problem within that sector.

Prior to 2007, many money market managers were probably not as concerned with what was happening on the swaps desk as they would be, or better said, should be today. The question was most certainly always raised, how the current swap activity would affect or change any decisions on what commercial paper to buy or how would it directly affect the short-term issues already owned. Maybe it is that the markets are much more correlated, as activity impacts each sector more directly. Or possibly, asset managers are that much smarter today because we have all lived through the market disruptions and activity. Either way, the stronger asset managers are keeping closer tabs on any sector that has the ability to disrupt or impact their positions.

Yes, I do think any asset manager who has successfully made it through the recent years of bank closures, government bailouts, and market disruptions has learned many lessons. Asset managers today should have the attitude and view that anything is possible, and as I mentioned early on in this book, expect the unexpected. Hold that statement close to you heart, because what you don't prepare for will likely hurt you. The markets are tightly linked, and that needs to be a starting point that creates an analysis broad enough to capture any disruption or dislocation within the markets.

The starting point on my road map is finding the right tools to help guide and answer any questions that come my way. I always start with the 10,000-foot view and work my way down. There are two ways to accomplish this. You either need to find a broad metric that helps telegraph the points that are needed to start your assessment, or to create a customized model or sentiment index. There is no question that finding an already-existing index or model is easier, but one potential problem is that it may not provide the exact information you are looking for. There may be a crucial piece missing. If you are lucky enough to find one that captures the pieces you are targeting, it will save you many hours of construction and updating. Ultimately, if you have the necessary time or you are looking to target a specific sector or section of the economy, a custom model is likely to provide the best result.

Figure 7.1 represents one of the two sentiment indicators that I created and look at daily. It is based on various metrics that help telegraph the fixed income landscape. It goes without saying that any model should not be used in isolation. It provides the starting blocks, and when combined with fundamental research, analysis, and instinct, helps form the necessary tools to help create or maintain your asset allocation. A benefit of using different models and various types of tools is that they add a nonemotional element to the mix, helping formulate views and ultimately, decisions.

This model captures broad market indicators, which are weighted accordingly, to provide a snapshot of the general health of the fixed income market. More specifically, through design, it captures a few volatility metrics that help portray the tone of the market. At the 10,000-foot level, it is important to use indicators that capture the breadth of the market. A

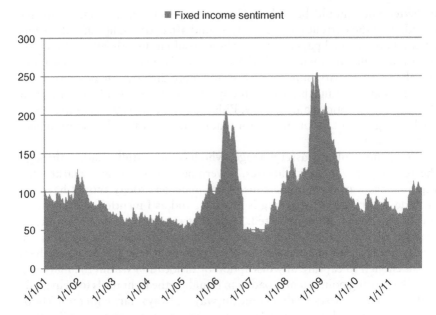

FIGURE 7.1   Fixed Income Sentiment Index Measuring Volatility
Source: Bloomberg data, Barclays Capital data.

too-specific or detailed input is not appropriate. To gain a sense of the broader market, I chose to use a combination of both equity and fixed income statistics. Historically, the model or index shows a strong record of representing turning points within the fixed income markets. Index peaks back in early 2006 and early 2009 represent the start of a massive move tighter in spreads and a march to a healthier market environment.

Carving out the time span from the fourth quarter of 2006 to the third quarter of 2007, we see in the model that the fixed income markets were complacent and looking frothy. At that point in time, the housing market bubble was stretched to extremes, ready to pop. Spreads were at unwarranted tight levels, and risk was abundant, even though it was perceived not to be. Clearly, caution needed to be taken. The model is not a crystal ball and does not forecast an exact turning point. A model such as this one requires you to use your skill set and knowledge of the current environment to add to the data the model provides.

Fast forward two years. The market continues to regress back toward the mean. Barring any exogenous event, at this point in time we would expect the fixed income market to remain healthy, anticipating further tightening within credit markets as the broader market continues to normalize.

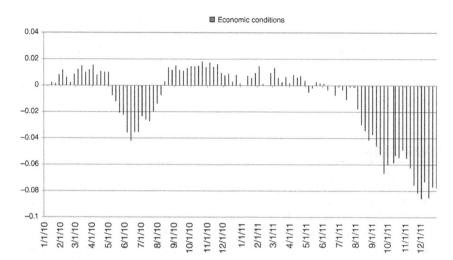

FIGURE 7.2 Economic Climate Index
Source: Bloomberg data; the Association of American Railroads, http://www.aar.
org/NewsAndEvents/Freight-Rail-Traffic.aspx.

To navigate through the turbulent sea of indicators while piecing together the broad yet intertwined data points, I utilize not only the fixed income sentiment model but also another sentiment index that closely tracks economic activity. Figure 7.2 adds another piece to the puzzle as it captures on a timely basis the release of various economic indicators and tracks their progress. This model, combined with the other, provides a deeper technical view of the market landscape.

An economic model used with the market sentiment model sets forth a clearer picture for you to make decisions. The combination of the models allows you to see a picture not only of market sentiment, but also the economy, and how one might drive the other.

The history over the past two years proved to be a challenge for the U.S. economy. There were plenty of false starts before the data gained traction, finally taking hold in the first quarter of 2012. The model shows what looks like a bottom in mid-November 2011. Support was found, as there were two attempts to move lower before the sharp move higher that commenced over the subsequent weeks.

There is no doubt that the U.S. economy has embarked on the road to recovery over the past few years. It has been a choppy ride, with different sectors taking turns on providing multiple starts, stops, and at times what felt like false hope. There are many differing views on the path ahead, but as the models show, the path looks bright. The economy and global markets will all play roles in the outcome of the journey. The task at hand is laying the groundwork to successfully reach the endgame. The game plan will need to be able to face different markets with periods of stabilization and bouts of turmoil thrown in the mix. The best way to navigate the markets and uncharted areas is with the right mix of sectors and securities. This is accomplished through asset allocation.

GOING GLOBAL

One goal of asset allocation is to reduce systemic risk. Proper asset allocation will help mitigate risk, but it will not remove it completely from your portfolio. Let's be honest here: If the global economy is slowing and on the fringe of entering a recession, the U.S. markets and those abroad will trade in similar fashion. That is to say, they'll trade lower as well. In that case, diversification will allow the portfolio to receive the varying degrees of negative returns, which may help the portfolio stay ahead of where it would have been if investing in only one or two asset classes. That is the goal. What investors have going for them today is the availability of global strategies right at their fingertips. Developed or emerging markets, or a combination of both, are much easier to implement today through a mutual fund or in a separate account structure than it was 20 years ago. North America—that is, Canada and the United States—accounts for approximately 28 percent of global gross domestic product (GDP).[1] That means that 72 percent of GDP comes from other regions. That fact alone should provide enough fodder to drive any manager to diversify a portfolio globally.

When striving for consistent long-term results, it is imperative to utilize all possible levers. By opening the portfolio borders, you give yourself a fighting chance for success. This is witnessed in monthly total returns between the Barclays Capital U.S. Aggregate index and the Barclays Capital Global Aggregate index ex-USD. Figure 7.3 shows a low correlation between the two. In the period beginning in 2005, these indexes carry a 58 percent correlation, even with the globalization of economies and growing intertwined markets. This low correlation is usually a welcome feature when you are looking to diversify. In the chart there are times when the two indexes move in similar fashion. It is also clear that the global markets do not always move in tandem with the U.S. market. Geopolitical events and different business

---

[1]USDA Economic Research Service, "International Macroeconomic Data Set," updated July 5, 2012, http://www.ers.usda.gov/data-products/international-macroeconomic-data-set.aspx.

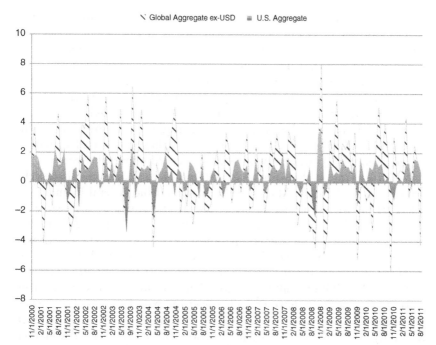

FIGURE 7.3 Correlation between Barclays Global Aggregate Index ex-USD and the Barclays Capital Aggregate Index.
Source: Barclays Capital Index data.

cycles are two of many drivers that usually have a hand in creating different results.

Ultimately, the purpose of asset allocation is to reduce risk within your portfolio. Different combinations of assets or sectors will attempt to provide different results through the changing market environments. Asset allocation is as simple as investing in multiple asset classes that, over time, have provided low correlation to one another. Cash, stocks, and bonds are the most basic way to diversify through asset allocation. It shouldn't stop at this level. Today's investing environment allows investors to achieve an even greater mix of assets through specialty mutual funds or unique separate account strategies.

Here is a simple yet effective example of how risk may be reduced not only through investing with different asset classes, but if taken yet another step in an attempt to further reduce risk within an asset class. The agency sector is one that many investors probably don't give the proper time of day in preparation for placing a trade. It is a known fact is that this sector carries the implied guarantee of the U.S. government. For some investors, the analysis may stop there because these securities carry that implied government guarantee . I disagree with that approach. Remember, the government has the ability to change the rules whenever it feels it is necessary. At any point in time, it can phase out or modify the implicit guarantee. A phase-out is probably not likely to happen without proper warning. Even with warning, once that news hits the tape, the sector will underperform as spreads blow out. The news doesn't have to be this drastic to cause headaches for investors within the sector. Headlines as simple as minor restructuring or increased regulation have the ability to create a nervous buzz that could impact the sector.

I will focus on the three primary, well-known companies that issue debt within the sector: Fannie Mae, Freddie Mac, and the Federal Home Loan Bank (FHLB). The agency sector historically trades with a tight spread over and above the U.S. Treasury sector. In "normal" market conditions, the spread or additional yield over comparable Treasury for the 10-year agency may fall between 25 and 65 basis points (bps). The Bloomberg Fair Value 10-year index shows an average spread of 55 bps from January 2000 through December 2011. It is difficult to classify what is normal, because a turbulent environment appears to have prevailed over the past 10 years. Turbulence and uncertainty don't have to be present within the sector. Direct or indirect uncertainty affects the spread and price action within the sector. The market doesn't play favorites, but investors do. The outcome within the sector isn't always the same for each security—in this case the agencies. Historically, the spreads of the three primary agency issuers trade within a narrow margin of each other. This isn't always the case. The details that surround the company's book of business, or exposure and the support for their debt, are key drivers for how the issued debt will perform. Varying circumstances, positive or negative, create different opportunities as well as price action.

Investors within this sector have had to wrestle with the ongoing balance sheet concerns of Fannie Mae, Freddie Mac, and the FHLB. Investors have focused more heavily on Fannie Mae and Freddie Mac due to their structure. Complicating matters is the continual threat of the government removing the implied guarantee that investors demand. If the government pulled its implied guarantee, there would be severe ramifications to the sector. Fannie Mae and Freddie Mac are perceived to have the closest ties to the government and would be impacted the hardest if the aforementioned events occurred (that is, with all else being equal). The FHLB might not be as affected due to its structure, with 12 regional federal home loan banks that are each supported by one another through a cooperative ownership. [2] This is a key

---

[2]FHL Banks homepage, www.fhlbanks.com.

difference from the other agencies. The ownership structure is looked at as additional support. Proper analysis would view the ownership structure as the primary piece and the governmental support the backup or additional layer of comfort. If problems arise within the agency sector, the FHLB debt will likely underperform in sympathy. As headlines rock the agency sector, pushing spreads wider and prices lower, the increased support and structural differences help the securities' overall performance. This would be one of those situations where I would look to add exposure on a dislocation. Similar to the corporate sector, different securities within the agency sector may perform differently.

Over the past three years, the threat of imminent default was not a concern with any of the aforementioned issuers. Investors have had to deal with reduced liquidity and wider bid-ask spreads. Wider bid-ask spreads and reduced liquidity helped formulate my opinion about the sector. When I was involved in the sector over the past few years, I regularly favored the FHLB over the other issuers. At times, I may have had exposure elsewhere, as the goal was to find the relative value and diversify within the sector.

Just remember that regardless of the shape of the yield curve or the sector allocation, the landscape and need for asset allocation are always evolving. The lesson learned over the past few years is that all markets are intertwined with each other in more ways than are imaginable. Not only does the financial system need to be healed, but so do the balance sheets of corporations and households alike.

For these reasons and many others, a broader view of the fixed income market needs to be taken, capturing a variety of metrics broad enough— yet acutely interrelated—to provide an accurate representation. Instinct will always play a key role in assessing the market, although proper tools will provide an edge. This edge will help dissect the key components within the fixed income market. The technical view will remove the emotional aspect of investing, allowing the data points to be looked at as just that: data points. These raw data will then be used in conjunction with fundamental analysis and instinct to help anticipate the ever-evolving fixed income landscape and remain ahead of the curve.

CHAPTER 8

The Federal Reserve and Central Banks

Achieving price stability is not only important in itself, it is also central to attaining the Federal Reserve's other mandate objectives of maximum sustainable employment and moderate long-term interest rates.

—Ben Bernanke

The Federal Open Market Committee (FOMC) was established by the Banking Act of 1933 and is comprised of 12 members. Investors within the fixed income and equity markets know that the FOMC is responsible for setting monetary policy. Monetary policy is a term that gets thrown around many different ways.

The classic definition provided by the Federal Reserve is as follows:

The term "monetary policy" refers to the actions undertaken by a central bank, such as the Federal Reserve, to influence the availability and cost of money and credit to help promote national economic goals.

The FOMC is responsible for carrying a dual mandate on its shoulders. Many investors, including myself, feel that the committee is burdened with conflicting principles in that dual mandate. Responsibilities of the committee include the promotion of economic growth or maximum employment while holding inflation in check and keeping prices stable. As you can imagine, this balance is an ongoing tug-of-war; too much money in circulation contributes to inflationary pressures. Recent years have provided the committee a "get out of jail free card." The free pass was the prolonged low headline inflation level. Because inflation remained out of the picture, the committee was able to move freely on its best ideas in an attempt to spur economic growth.

Historically the committee uses the federal funds rate as a key tool in an attempt to stimulate growth. More recently, the committee has embarked on new and unconventional methods, including a coordinated effort with other central banks around the world. It is true that uncertain times call for uncertain measures. Without a doubt that adage applies here.

HAWKS AND DOVES

Hawks and doves aside, it all revolves around the fed funds rate. Voting members are sometimes classified as hawks if they are prone to vote for higher interest rates. Doves on the committee are those individuals who are less likely to carry a motion to raise interest rates. There is always a lot of discussion about who stands on which side of the line. At the end of the day, the ultimate decision on whether to change the fed funds rate falls on the chairman's shoulders. That decision is made at one of the committee's eight scheduled meetings, which usually occur on Tuesdays. The committee has the ability to meet at any point in time to change monetary policy, something we have witnessed in the past, although unscheduled meetings are rare. The last time an unscheduled meeting occurred was October 8, 2008, a few weeks after the demise of Lehman Brothers. Interestingly, the committee actually had a scheduled meeting the day following the Lehman bankruptcy, but the members opted against policy change, deciding not to lower the overnight rates at that time. The Reserve Fund, a money market mutual fund and a staple within the industry, announced that it was shutting down that same day, rocking the markets. Then, at their unscheduled meeting on October 8, the FOMC lowered interest rates from 2 percent to 1.5 percent at the unscheduled meeting, and again to 1 percent 21 days later. Emergency meetings usually occur, just as the name implies, in times of an emergency. The committee tries not to succumb to these types of meetings, as they have a tendency to create a negative tone with investors. Any time the FOMC makes an unscheduled policy change without providing investors prior transparency or notification, the committee risks damaging its credibility.

THE FED FUNDS RATE

The FOMC uses the federal funds rate as a tool to either add or remove accommodation. For instance, to curb inflation, the committee makes its policy more restrictive. One way to accomplish this is to remove accommodation by tightening policy and raising the overnight lending rate. When there is too little money in the banking system, credit is tight—that is, banks are unwilling to lend—and the FOMC's mandate is to promote growth. One strategy for accomplishing this is to adopt a less-restrictive policy. An example of becoming more accommodative is lowering the overnight lending rate and ultimately, putting more cash in the system. When this is accomplished, borrowing rates look more attractive to consumers and corporations, creating the willingness to borrow. Borrowing at these low rates, or at any rate for that matter, will stimulate money flow. This is looked at as taking an accommodative stance, which will help kick-start the economy. The goal is to increase the availability of credit, ultimately increasing the amount of money in circulation. In theory, this sounds foolproof. The more cash in the system, the greater amount of lending that will occur. One hurdle the Fed has had to deal with that is out of its control is that it can't control financial institutions' willingness to lend. It doesn't matter how cheap or accessible funds are; if banks are not willing to lend, growth will not occur. This was witnessed in the quarters and years after the housing bubble popped, when mortgage rates were driven by accommodative policy to historically low levels. Low rates didn't matter when consumers were not approved for loans. Banks were sitting on the cash, choosing to rebuild their balance sheets, which didn't help spur economic growth.

A SHORT-TERM FIXED INCOME INVESTOR

To a front-end investor, the fed funds rate is the starting point of a strategy. It is the core or center of the universe for many strategies. Securities used by portfolio managers to invest within these fixed income strategies are priced off or compared to the fed funds rate. Interest rate calls are also developed based off of intuitive thought process and models that utilize the rate. Historically, the spread between the target fed funds rate and the two-year Treasury is approximately 41 basis points. Any increase or decrease in spread could signal a change, impacting the strategy. If the spread narrows to 20 basis points and holds that range while the economy shows signs of expanding, the two-year may start to sell off in anticipation of Fed action. Without becoming consumed by detail, this is one example of how to utilize the fed funds rate and current spread to assist in your asset management process.

HOOKED ON ACCOMMODATION

History shows that the Federal Reserve has worked wonders to provide support to the market, creating a positive environment while at times crushing it shortly thereafter. With the turbulence and recent unexpected slowdown, the markets have tightened their reliance on Fed activity in recent years. Federal Reserve policy accommodation has become the markets' drug of choice. Almost systematically, when the equity market is feeling low, participants look to the Fed for a shot of accommodation. The fixed income markets are not excluded from the party either.

Policy accommodation takes many shapes. The committee lowered the U.S. overnight lending rate to a range of zero to 25 basis points (bps) in December 2008. It then embarked on multiple iterations of quantitative easing (QE) measures to provide support when needed and spur on the economy. Most recently, Operation Twist directly impacted the fixed income markets. In Operation Twist the Fed repositioned its balance sheet by selling short-dated holdings and using the proceeds to purchase longer-dated securities. This activity from the Fed did not inject new cash into the system, but was only the reallocation of existing positions within its portfolio along the yield curve. The FOMC successfully helped fuel another leg of the U.S. Treasury market rally.

The support provided by the Fed is unlikely to end for many years to come. The web is woven deep within the economy and investor sentiment. Policy action may take different shapes in upcoming years. Investors also should realize that the markets will remain supported by central bank activity and the expectation of future U.S. economic and global growth. Central banks around the world have embarked on various forms of stimulus. The European Central Bank (ECB) last lowered its overnight rate by 25 bps in December 2011. The Bank of England (BOE) lowered its base lending rate to 50 basis points in March of 2009. Both the ECB and BOE provided investors with subsequent stimulus plans, helping to support the global financial system. The consensus view has moved back and forth on whether the eurozone is likely to enter into a recession, adding additional uncertainty to the already tenuous situation. If another recession is in the eurozone's cards, will it pull the U.S. economy down with it? These uncertainties have created the case for additional support from the ECB and BOE. It has also required the Fed to remain on guard, ready to provide the next round of accommodation if necessary.

DEPOSITS WITH CENTRAL BANKS

Investors globally are always trying figure out how to stay in front of central bank activity. What is the most accurate way to gauge the central bank's next move and its impact on the markets? Unfortunately, there is no clear-cut way to get into the chiefs' heads. The task at hand first requires an understanding of why the central bank is creating easy money. Most recently, the central banks globally have been fighting two battles that feed off each other. The fear or reality of a global slowdown is amplified by the support needed within the banking system. These two crises, for lack of a better word, are difficult enough to handle individually, but when combined as a one-two punch, create a daunting task. We know that bank balance sheets need to be capitalized. Ratios need to be increased and stress tests passed. I look to different indicators to track the progress of funding needs. The stress or perceived stress in the markets is crucial to track as well. Financial stress has a dilapidating effect on financial institutions. One way to measure the amount of stress is to count the number of individuals standing in line in front of the bank waiting to transfer all their hard-earned assets from the bank into their mattress. Although that might be a true measure of stress, you are probably too late to the party to uncover the problem. There are better tools for measuring financial stress. One indicator I look to is the ECB Eurozone Liquidity Recourse to the Deposit Facility index. Put simply, this is the amount of funds institutions have on loan overnight with the ECB. Different investors may interpret this in different ways. I use it as an indicator of stress within the markets. The larger the amount banks have on loan with the ECB, the greater uncertainty they have with each other. All other things being equal, if financial institutions are comfortable giving up yield by lending overnight to the central bank instead of to each other, there is reason for caution. High amounts on loan don't necessarily mean a collapse within the system is imminent, but any elevated data are worth noting to uncover what is creating the abnormality. Figure 8.1 shows the increased use of the ECB for overnight lending. Approaching the end of the first quarter in 2012, assets on loan was hovering near the recent highs of 827 billion euros, hit on March 5. Average assets on loan for one year ending February 29, 2012, were 170.2 billion euros, compared to 123 billion euros for the prior year. This was an increase of just over 38 percent.

The jump in assets on loan corresponds with the second Long-Term Refinancing Operation (LTRO) extended to financial institutions by the government. That explains the large change, but the question remains: Why lend it back to the government when there are other opportunities for investment? Years of managing money have taught me to look for the negative, the tail risk, and in this case, that is the fact that institutions are leery of lending to each other. The environment leads investors to remain skeptical about each other's solvency. Whether there is government support or not, why take the chance of a possible default? If push comes to shove, the government is less likely to default. This specific example telegraphs how central banks will remain involved, providing support in the near term.

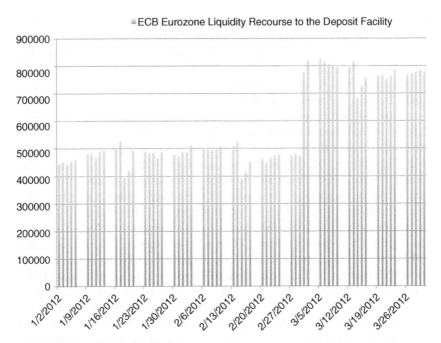

FIGURE 8.1   There Has Been a Recent Increase in Use of the Deposit Facility
Source: Bloomberg data.

WHAT ABOUT THE UNITED STATES?

Similar occurrences continue to take place within the U.S. markets. In conjunction with central bank activity around the world, Fed activity was taking place in the States. The following scenario sets the stage and lays the groundwork for the possibility of further Fed activity. The time period was from late 2011 to early 2012.

Fed rhetoric on balance remains dovish from the current lineup of voting members. This should not be a surprise, because U.S. economic data ebb and flow from showing signs of strength to signs of weakness. The ongoing question running through our minds was will the Fed commence on QE3, and if so, when? The FOMC had already implemented two rounds of quantitative easing through asset purchase plans. Round one was initiated on November 25, 2008, shortly after the demise of Lehman Brothers and the Reserve Fund. Round two commenced on November 3, 2010, and ran through June of the following year, with less of an effect on the markets.

The FOMC has two scheduled meetings early in the year. The first quarter of 2012 was too early in the year for the Fed to embark on additional accommodation or asset purchases at either of these meetings. The data points weren't troubling enough, but they weren't strong enough either, which is why the Fed remained sidelined for some time. A new process is that the Fed unveils the much-anticipated forecasts from each participant on when the Fed will raise interest rates. It will also disclose each participant's view of what the appropriate fed funds level will be at the end of the subsequent years. It is likely, however, that chairman Bernanke will reiterate that QE3 is still a viable option for many meetings to come. A case is being made for additional stimulus, and if the economic conditions do not show signs of improvement or take another step backwards, QE3 rhetoric may become reality in the second half of the year. If correct, the view on interest rates will remain low due to the accommodative stance. I watched for additional clues out of the Fed's meetings this year in attempt to get a sense of the line drawn in the sand. Time after time, Chairman Bernanke's comments kept pointing in the right direction. That direction was easy money through accommodative policy. Based on the view that rates will remain low for some time, it was more pertinent than ever to tune out the daily headlines and near-term volatility and remain disciplined. Staying long and overweighting sectors that benefit from an accommodative policy paid off. In addition to any alpha generated, trading costs were avoided by holding current positions and looking to market time.

The front end of the yield curve, including the money market sector, remains locked in place for the foreseeable future. Again, comments from committee members—including the chairman himself—clearly showed that it plans on holding interest rates exceptionally low for an extended time period. The committee clarified this further by stating rates will remain low through the end of 2014. Investors need to remember that these forecasts, along with any new transparency the committee embarks on, are just that: forecasts. They are not set in stone and can be adjusted as the economic climate shifts. With that said, the committee does not want to lose credibility with investors; therefore, it will be very cautious if changes are to be made. Changes within statements will need to be methodically thought out and scripted so as not to jolt the market. Futures are painting an even different picture. Fed funds futures show the Fed, as always, has an out. Futures are pricing in the removal of accommodation before the end of 2014, but not for multiple quarters. Supporting this view was the cap placed on LIBOR due to the various lifelines central banks have implemented. Combine these data points, an intuitive thought process, and the different sentiment indexes described earlier in this chapter and you can see how all these pieces form a clear picture of the activity of the Fed and its impact within the markets.

FOMC: LOOK FOR CLUES FROM
THE FED STATEMENT

We know that the Fed meets eight times a year. At these meetings, it can adjust monetary policy if and when the committee feels there is a need. Investors are always trying to get the upper edge through analysis of the markets and comments from the members of the FOMC. Needless to say, Fed rhetoric and Fed activity play a role with the markets. The relationship between the FOMC and the markets is strong. For this reason, it is very important for you to have a strong understanding of its view at all times. Aside from following member speeches on a daily basis, consult the FOMC statement to investors after each of its eight scheduled meetings. If they happen to have an unscheduled meeting, a statement is provided then as well. The statements or assessments provide an update of the current market conditions through opinions and forecasts on the current state of the economy and overall economic growth. This is why it is important to look for clues from the Fed statement that will provide guidance on which way interest rates are likely to move. We know that there is not a 100 percent guarantee, particularly in the near term, on the direction of interest rates. Over the long run, the Fed statement should be a helpful guide to assess the economy, current interest rate environment, and future direction of interest rates.

The Federal Reserve is one of the most influential—if not the most, influential—governing body that affects the markets. Two points come to mind when I think about the FOMC. The committee has a purpose and a goal, two similar, yet very distinct concepts. The primary purpose of the committee is to set monetary policy, and we also know its actions are to promote growth and control inflation.

The Fed always has the same endgame in sight, regardless of the direction in which interest rates are moving. The goal is to balance economic growth and inflation, and as you can imagine, achieving that balance is an ongoing tug-of-war.

WHAT TO LOOK FOR FROM THE FED . . . CLUES?

The ability to dissect Fedspeak is a skill set that can take a lifetime to learn. Fedspeak is the wording and language that is unique to the varying commentaries and statements Fed officials present. Some of these statements are from voting members of the FOMC, but they are not limited to them alone. FOMC members, as well as other Fed officials, provide different types of commentary. Some of the statements are made within the context of the committee's view, whereas others are statements that are made on an individual basis, not representing a united view, but speaking on their own behalf. The statements usually are created to serve a purpose and present a piece of the puzzle. These presentations are crafted with meticulous precision, to provide investors enough information to help convey a point without giving the committee's hand away by providing too much information. Even though the Federal Reserve and FOMC seem like an enigma, their goal is to craft various statements in effort to guide the market and investors. Transparency and clarity are two characteristics that investors would like to believe are always in the speaker's mind when the speeches are written. More times than not, the commentary or rhetoric you hear is almost like listening to code. The statements are not that clear and transparent. They are written more like riddles.

Even after studying each and every statement and listening to hundreds of speeches specifically for clues over the years, I cannot stress enough that the statements the FOMC provides are written as riddles.

FOMC STATEMENT: AUGUST 2011

Here is an example of what I was looking for from the August 2011 FOMC statement. This is a piece that I wrote one morning before the meeting.

Today is the first of two critical platforms where the FOMC chairman Bernanke will hold the spotlight. Today's FOMC meeting and the Jackson Hole Summit that starts August 26 will provide ample opportunities for the Fed to provide guidance to the markets. There is no doubt that policy intervention will help calm the global markets. Unfortunately, at this point in time, intervention in the form of QE3 is unlikely to occur.

The communication from the committee is the core goal today. The message that should be disseminated is the committee has a game plan to help stabilize the recent turmoil in the equity markets and economy. The problem the Fed is dealing with is the lack of ammunition. Absent from embarking on another outright buying program, which in my view is miles away, the committee needs to indicate it will be responsive if the situation continues to weaken. This is also where the Fed walks a fine line between calming the market and potentially adding disruption to the market, portraying the economy as worse off than it actually is.

One goal is to move rates as low as possible and create stability within the system. (The committee has been successful regarding the first part.) This will help with liquidity and ultimately build confidence with the end goal of stimulating the economy. The problem is it does not solve one of the largest troubles facing our economy—the creation of jobs.

I look for the Fed to provide guidance that it is ready to step in with stimulus if the environment continues to deteriorate. As usual, it will provide an assessment of the economy, touching on the decrease in energy prices, oil in particular, which is a positive for consumers. Last, the committee will touch on the recent action within the global equity markets with the hope to calm investors.

The key points to look for from the statement are:

- Mention of QE3
- Calming statements for investors
- Committee awareness of the current situation

Here is the statement from the August 8 meeting. This is a typical statement that the FOMC releases after each meeting. There is one paragraph that discusses the economic landscape, one for current policy and one for future policy. These statements can be found on the Federal Reserve's website www.federalreserve.gov. Here is the transcript from the August 9, 2011, statement.

Information received since the Federal Open Market committee met in June indicates that economic growth so far this year has been considerably slower than the Committee had expected. Indicators suggest a deterioration in overall labor market conditions in recent months, and the unemployment rate has moved up. Household spending has flattened out, investment in nonresidential structures is still weak, and the housing sector remains depressed. However, business investment in equipment and software continues to expand. Temporary factors, including the damping effect of higher food and energy prices on consumer purchasing power and spending as well as supply chain disruptions associated with the tragic events in Japan, appear to account for only some of the recent weakness in economic activity. Inflation picked up earlier in the year, mainly reflecting higher prices for some commodities and imported goods, as well as the supply chain disruptions. More recently, inflation has moderated as prices of energy and some commodities have declined from their earlier peaks. Longer-term inflation expectations have remained stable.

Consistent with its statutory mandate, the Committee seeks to foster maximum employment and price stability. The Committee now expects a somewhat slower pace of recovery over coming quarters than it did at the time of the previous meeting and anticipates that the unemployment rate will decline only gradually toward levels that the Committee judges to be consistent with its dual mandate. Moreover, downside risks to the economic outlook have increased. The Committee also anticipates that inflation will settle, over coming quarters, at levels at or below those consistent with the Committee's dual mandate as the effects of past energy and other commodity price increases dissipate further. However, the Committee will continue to pay close attention to the evolution of inflation and inflation expectations.

To promote the ongoing economic recovery and to help ensure that inflation, over time, is at levels consistent with its mandate, the Committee decided today to keep the target range for the federal funds rate at 0 to .25 percent. The Committee currently anticipates that economic conditions—including low rates of resource utilization and a subdued outlook for inflation over the medium run—are likely to warrant exceptionally low levels for the federal funds rate at least through mid-2013. The Committee also will maintain its existing policy of reinvesting principal payments from its securities holdings. The Committee will regularly review the size and composition of its securities holdings and is prepared to adjust those holdings as appropriate.

The Committee discussed the range of policy tools available to promote a stronger economic recovery in a context of price stability. It will continue to assess the economic outlook in light of incoming information and is prepared to employ these tools as appropriate.

Voting for the FOMC monetary policy actions were: Ben S. Bernanke, Chairman; William C. Dudley, Vice Chairman; Elizabeth A. Duke; Charles L. Evans; Sarah Bloom Raskin; Daniel K. Tarullo; and Janet L. Yellen.

Voting against the action were: Richard W. Fisher, Narayana Kocherlakota, and Charles I. Plosser, who would have preferred to continue to describe conditions as likely to warrant exceptionally low levels for the federal funds rate for an extended period.

Upon review of the statement, clues were uncovered that shed additional light on the Fed's view of the economy. The committee provided minor downgrades that offset any inferred upgrade language. The statement market participants focused on was the change in language on how long rates would remain at these exceptionally low levels. Prior to this statement, the Fed had continued to reuse a phrase that described its view on the timing of the fed funds rate. Any change to the funds rate would affect the overall interest rate environment. Statement after statement the committee hammered home the phrase "exceptionally low levels for the federal funds rate for an extended period." Most participants took this to mean rates would remain low indefinitely. The problem the Fed had to face was that clarity about the timing or—a specific date—was what many investors were looking for.

The committee delivered the message to investors. Although it was not a unanimous decision, the Fed policy-setting committee did alter the phrase with the key words "exceptionally low" and "extended period," replacing them with a more concrete date. Chairman Bernanke and his committee members committed to hold the fed funds rate at low levels at least through mid-2013. This change was significant, providing the clarity to fixed income and equity investors alike. This statement anchored the front end, as it is tethered to Fed policy. The initial knee-jerk reaction of risk markets, such as non-government sectors, was to sell off the following day. This move was short lived, as the Dow Jones Industrial average reversed its course, surpassing the pre-announcement levels that printed earlier in the week. This change provided the ammunition investors were looking for, while providing a calming message that the Fed was going to remain vigilant and do whatever it needed to do in efforts to keep the economy on a growth trajectory.

QE OR NOT QE

There were no changes to its balance sheet. That translates into, "At the time, no additional quantitative easing is in store." That didn't mean it was off the table altogether; the committee was likely saving its bullets in case the economy did not improve at the speed that it felt it should. The additional language did provide a calming effect on investors.

CALMING STATEMENTS FOR INVESTORS

Statements such as "downside risks to economic outlook increased and labor market indicators suggest deterioration" set the tone. Calming? I don't think so. If any statement had the chance to be considered calming it would have been that "inflation has moderated." Investors should have interpreted this to mean that the Fed had a green light and the engine was running hot. Low inflation signals that the chairman is standing ready to turn on the printing press and do whatever it takes, even if that means expanding its balance sheet, to help out the economy.

Last, the committee did send the signal that it was on top of the ongoing and ever-changing situation. A little reassurance goes a long way. Investors— including myself—are more willing to put money to work when we feel that the Fed is on top of the situation. I may not agree with the Fed and its decisions, but I can manage around that. It is the unknown that derails the market and dampens investor sentiment. Chairman Bernanke did address, in one fashion or another, the three pieces that I was looking for. The statement was not straightforward but the pieces were there.

CHAPTER 9

The Economy and the Markets

Economics is a subject that does not greatly respect one's wishes.
—Nikita Khrushchev

There are numerous data points and economic indicators that investors and market participants follow. Some are relevant and others are not. As is always the case, the landscape becomes even more complicated when the fixed income market is involved in the equation. The complexity can be seen as unfortunate or fortunate, depending on how you view the markets and the world of investing. Globalization of the fixed income arena and economy over the past decades has added new twists and turns that investors need to navigate. As a result, it is easy to immerse yourself in data points that, at times, can become very overwhelming.

There are economists and strategists who probably follow almost every data point that the economy and markets throw at them. Chances are, it is vital for a short-term trader to track and analyze numerous data points. Long-term investors may follow another path. Economic data points have the ability to create short-term volatility, which leads to dislocations. Traders thrive on dislocations, which create money-making opportunities. This is a good time to emphasize again that as a portfolio manager, you should consider and plan each trade for the long haul. As I said in prior chapters, create your road map. This is one key difference between trading and investing.

When the approach taken is investing, it is my strategy to narrow the list of economic indicators to follow and focus on key reports that have the ability to alter the market's long-term outcome. Throw out the noise and second-tier indicators and focus on what is important. The emphasis should be on indicators that have the ability to directly move the market, but you have to be careful with this. Every indicator, first-tier or otherwise, has the ability to create a knee-jerk reaction and move the market in the near term. Traders large and small add fuel to the knee-jerk reaction as they try to gain positioning for a possible momentum trade. The intelligent move, for lack of a better phrase, is to look for the indicators that have the ability to change the markets and impact your strategy over the long term. The next section of this chapter outlines market indicators that have the ability to shape and influence the long-term investor's portfolio.

To start, an economic indicator is a data point that represents a group of data points that describe how well the economy or business sector is doing. These indicators are released at various frequencies—weekly, monthly, and sometimes, quarterly. Common sense tells you that the greater the frequency of a report, the fresher or better the sample of data on the economy that will be produced. This gets tricky, because you need to be able to ignore the noise that is sometimes associated with data points that are released on a more frequent basis. Take, for example, the jobless claims report, which is released weekly. Due to the frequency, added volatility may be introduced. Outside events such as holidays or inclement weather conditions can affect the data, as individuals may be influenced.

However you look at it, the economy has a direct impact on investing, which is why it is so important to find a set of data points to follow and religiously track. The reoccurring question is, which to follow? More times than not, the data points that you hear about on TV or read about in various journals have the most noise around them. These probably do not have the most impact on your portfolio over the long term. I refer to these points as second-tier data points. It is almost impossible to follow each and every point with skill unless you devote every day to the analysis. The solution for most is to have some sort of working knowledge of the data points. Even then, it is difficult to capture all the necessary aspects of the data.

It is easy to get inundated by all the data points that are presented within the market, losing track of what is really important. I am not suggesting that you ignore market and economic indicators; what I am suggesting is to follow in depth the ones that count. Follow the indicators that have the potential to move the market and impact your portfolio strategy over the long term. Taking that a step further: Follow those indicators that are top tier and have the ability to move or shift long-term market expectations and direction. This group of indicators will provide in-depth insight to the market. Although I closely follow numerous data points, if you do not have a full day to track and analyze economic figures, there are four data points that are essential and provide the power to move the fixed income world.

Each touches and impacts the broader market in one way. The four valuable data points are as follows:

1. Employment picture—Nonfarm payroll data, continuing claims (not the weekly jobless claims)
2. Inflation picture—Consumer price index, personal consumption expenditure
3. Consumption data—Consumer spending, retail sales
4. Interest rate environment—The actions of the FOMC

THE PAYROLL PICTURE: THE BACKBONE TO THE ECONOMY

The nonfarm payroll data present one of the best snapshots on the health of the labor market. This indicator is also very influential within the fixed income markets. Due to its influence, it also plays an important role in shedding light for investors to assess the overall economy. This can be taken a step further and used to measure the health of the individual consumer.

BUREAU OF LABOR STATISTICS WEBSITE

Before we go any further, let's look at how the establishment payroll survey is defined.

On its website (http://www.bls.gov/ces/cesfaq.htm#scope1), the Bureau of Labor Statistics describes the current employment statistics (CES) survey as follows:

> *The establishment payroll survey, known as the current employment statistics survey, is based on a survey of approximately 141,000 business and government agencies representing approximately 486,000 worksites throughout the United States. The primary statistics derived from the survey are monthly estimates of employment, hours, and earnings for the nation, states, and major metropolitan areas. Preliminary national estimates for a given reference month are typically released on the third Friday after the conclusion of the reference week; i.e., the week which includes the 12th of the month, in conjunction with data derived from a separate survey of households, the current population survey (CPS). CES employment is an estimate of the number of nonfarm, payroll jobs in the U.S.*

*economy. Employment is the total number of persons on estab-
lishment payrolls employed full- or part-time who received pay for
any part of the pay period that includes the 12th day of the month.
Temporary and intermittent employees are included, as are any
employees who are on paid sick leave, on paid holiday, or who
work during only part of the specified pay period.*

In the simplest terms, the nonfarm payroll report measures the number
of jobs that are created within the private and public sector. Jobs within the
private sector are nongovernmental jobs, and governmental jobs represent
the public sector. I consider the payroll report a top-tier indicator. As noted
previously, the data points provide great insight, impacting not only the
fixed income markets, but also the equity markets, commodity markets, and
the dollar.

The nonfarm payroll report is not the only measure of job creation.
There are other employment releases that capture job creation. Some of
these releases are respectable and others, in my opinion, fall short. Or at the
very least, the reports are not consistent or do not paint the entire picture,
leaving gaps that could hinder your analysis. The nonfarm payroll report
has a sister report that is also released on a monthly basis, known as the
ADP National Employment Report. According to Bloomberg:

*The ADP National Employment Report is a measure of nonfarm
private employment, based on a subset of aggregated and anony-
mous payroll data, using approximately 365,000 of the 500,000
U.S. business clients and approximately 24 million employees working in all 19 of the major North American Industrial Classification
private industrial sectors.*

The ADP Report is another piece of the labor puzzle. The report is
important in formulating a broad market view; on a stand-alone basis, I
view it as a second-tier report. The fact that the report excludes government
jobs does not allow the investor to receive the entire labor picture. Some
economists and analysts try to use this report as a forecaster for the BLS
nonfarm payroll report; however, its track record is less than stellar.

There is also a weekly new jobless claims report that comes out every
Thursday at 8:30 A.M. This report shows how many individuals are applying
or filing for unemployment benefits. This report has a history of being very
volatile, due to seasonal factors and factors such as weather, which may
hinder individuals from filing. As a result of the volatility, I look at this
indicator also as a second-tier indicator that must be taken at face value.
What is important is that you look at the trends and try to capture the overall

health of the labor market. One way to track this is to look at the 4-week moving average, which smooths out the volatility and noise. In addition to first-time benefits, another report released simultaneously shows those individuals who continue to file for benefits—the continuing claims report. Put all these reports together and you have now created a solid picture of the employment landscape. The problem is that if you are following all these various reports you have just spent a couple of hours analyzing them to become well-educated. Not to mention these reports are provided on different days. It would be too easy if they were released consecutively on the same day. For this reason, the nonfarm payroll report is the report to lean on for a snapshot of the labor environment.

The heart of labor market analysis is the nonfarm payroll report. It cannot be said enough that this report and its data is a phenomenal indicator to assess the health of the labor market, the economy, and in the end, the individual consumer. This data point is normally released at 8:30 A.M. on the first Friday of every month. This indicator signals if companies are in the hiring mode, and therefore, expanding and growing, which is of course a positive for the economy. A positive payroll number reflects a healthy or growing labor market. The opposite is true regarding a negative number. A negative or static number, depending on the environment, may show contraction and a deteriorating labor market.

A fading labor market is never a good sign. It will usually lead to a higher unemployment rate, which has its own list of implications. A high unemployment rate usually weighs on economic growth. A positive report will reflect whether companies are hiring and expanding their workforce. If they are expanding, it is likely in anticipation of stronger demand for the products they make or services they deliver. On the flip side, if companies are seeing sales start to decrease and expect less future demand, they are likely to reduce their workforce by laying off workers. These different scenarios can play havoc with the markets. A strong or soft release will immediately impact the markets and Treasury sector. Figure 9.1 represents the nonfarm payroll data dating back to 2002. You can see that this report can be volatile. Also take a close look at patterns that develop over the years. For instance, on average, December and June fall on the weaker side. Historically, May and October have tended to provide stronger results. It is important to look through the noise. Isolate those occurrences that happen in a recession and those that do not. These different time periods have the ability to produce varying results and differences. When analyzing the data, it is also important to consider and account for any exogenous factors. That sounds simple enough, pretty much stating the obvious. Due to the depth of your day-to-day analysis of the data, it is very easy to become handcuffed with tunnel vision, unaware of the changing surroundings.

Year	January	February	March	April	May	June	July	August	September	October	November	December
2002	-129	-146	-24	-84	-9	47	-100	-11	-55	121	8	-163
2003	95	-159	-213	-49	-9	0	25	-45	109	197	14	119
2004	162	44	337	249	310	81	46	122	166	348	63	134
2005	137	240	141	360	170	243	374	193	66	80	334	160
2006	283	316	283	181	14	76	209	183	157	-9	204	171
2007	236	93	190	72	139	75	-40	-18	73	79	112	89
2008	41	-84	-95	-208	-190	-198	-210	-274	-432	-498	-803	-661
2009	-818	-724	-799	-692	-361	-482	-339	-231	-199	-202	-42	-171
2010	-40	-35	189	239	516	-167	-58	-51	-27	220	121	120
2011	110	220	246	251	54	84	96	85	202	112	157	223
Average	7.70	-23.50	25.50	31.90	63.40	-24.10	0.30	-4.70	6.00	44.80	16.80	2.10
Average Nonrecession	106.75	71.63	143.63	152.38	148.13	54.875	23.67	25.22	54.67	105.11	107.89	74.13
Average Recession	-388.50	-404.00	-447.00	-450.00	-275.50	-340.00	-210.00	-274.00	-432.00	-498.00	-803.00	-661.00
Positive Numbers	70%	50%	60%	60%	60%	60%	50%	40%	60%	70%	80%	70%
Negative Numbers	30%	50%	40%	40%	40%	40%	50%	60%	40%	30%	20%	30%
Max	283	316	337	360	516	243	374	193	202	348	334	223
Min	-818	-724	-799	-692	-361	-482	-339	-274	-432	-498	-803	-661

FIGURE 9.1 Historical Non-Farm Payroll Data (P is preliminary)
Source: BLS.

Diving a little deeper into this report, there are multiple components that provide additional information on the health of the economy. A component that is worth noting, one that is followed by many investors and on which I place strong weight, is the temporary help category. This category is closely watched by money managers and economists, particularly when trying to assess future job growth. Market participants utilize this report quite heavily when assessing whether or not the economy is coming out of a recession. At the risk of contradicting myself, earlier, I mentioned to tune out what you hear on the market news channel to avoid becoming overwhelmed with superfluous data. If you turn on almost any financial news channel at 8:30 A.M. on the Friday the employment data are released, this is a piece of the nonfarm payroll you will hear about, and it is worth digesting.

Every investor, large or small, is always on the hunt for clues on what is to come: the crystal ball syndrome. Unfortunately, working crystal balls are hard to come by. The next best thing is to look for leading indicators within the economic release. An early signal of a recovery within the labor market can be gleaned from the temporary help category. A positive tick higher in the temporary help category may mean future growth within the sector. There are multiple reasons why an employer would rather hire an individual on a part-time basis than a full-time position. Arguments may range from cost savings in benefits to lack of consumer demand for the end product. Companies are more likely to hire temporary help before investing in a full-time employee. A rule of thumb I subscribe to is that there is a three- to six-month lag or transition from job growth within the temporary help category to when permanent jobs are created. Recently, the delay has become a little bit longer. This is the natural course of action. Companies will slowly ramp up their head count to meet demand through temporary employees, eventually shifting those positions into full-time positions to meet increased demand. You can see how and why the health of the labor market is a strong indicator of the overall health of the economy and ultimately the consumer. In the end, if the consumer is gainfully employed in a full-time position, they are more likely to open their wallet, helping fuel the economy.

Because the nonfarm payroll report has the potential to move markets, it is important to view it in conjunction with other sectors. Similar to other indicators, the nonfarm payroll data reveal patterns over time. As Figure 9.1 showed, four out of the last five sets of July payroll data (released the first week in August) have provided negative numbers. Table 9.1 shows the yield action within the Treasury sector. Focus on the 10-year Treasury for the month of August over the same five years we were looking at regarding the negative payroll prints. It is a strong move within the 10-year sector over that time horizon. Impacting the Treasury sector was the softer payroll print.

TABLE 9.1 10-year Treasury Action

	Start	End	Change
2007	4.79%	4.53%	−0.26%
2008	3.93%	3.81%	−0.12%
2009	3.63%	3.45%	−0.18%
2010	2.91%	2.65%	−0.26%
2011	2.62%	2.19%	−0.43%

Source: Bloomberg data.

It goes without saying that additional inputs or exogenous events also contributed to the rally in the Treasury market in August from 2007 to 2011. Yields fell on average 25 basis points (bps) over the five years. The front end of the yield curve had similar action. My data show that the two-year Treasury note rallied 75 percent of the time after the release of the July payroll data. This number may vary slightly, depending on the mark chosen from the prior day's closing price and the closing price on the payroll day. There was also one occurrence removed as the two-year was unchanged after the release. In any event, there is a strong case to be made on the ability of the nonfarm payroll number to move markets. The bottom line: As companies shed workers, in theory, the economy may start to struggle. When the economy struggles, there is usually a flight-to-quality trade that occurs in the Treasury market. Regardless of where we are in an economic cycle, the track record provides reason to be cautious in August regarding the July payroll print, and positive within the Treasury sector. These trends do not only occur in the summer; these types of anomalies happen on a daily basis and in almost every market. The trick is uncovering them and finding a way to profit from the dislocation.

One last note on the payroll data. The labor market is a key driver in the health of the economy. Think of it this way: When employed consumers generally feel happy and confident, they are more willing to go out and spend their paycheck. What happens if the consumer starts to lose interest in his or her job? Or what if confidence begins to wane and job security is now in question? In either scenario, common sense should tell you what needs to happen. You will likely start to reign in some of your spending. At the very least, reduce your discretionary spending and increase your savings. There is always the other side of the coin as well. A confident consumer will be less inclined to question or analyze their spending habits. Whichever side is chosen, the labor market will indirectly represent the consumer, corporations, and ultimately the economy. For this reason, the labor market, including the nonfarm payroll release, is a very powerful indicator and without a doubt, makes the top four indicators to monitor.

INFLATION: A FIXED INCOME INVESTOR'S ENEMY

What has the possibility of creating a headache for not only the Federal Reserve but investors and consumers alike? This is not a trick question. The answer is inflation. Inflation has the ability to erode your purchasing power. In the simplest terms, a dollar today is worth less tomorrow. Another way to look at it is that today, your dollar has the ability to purchase a candy bar. Six months or one year from now, or maybe even in two years, the same dollar may not be able to purchase the same candy bar. Or, if a dollar still buys a candy bar, the size of the bar might be noticeably smaller. That is inflation. There are a number of ways to measure inflation and inflationary pressures. The producer price index and consumer price index are straightforward, providing insight across almost all levels. These two reports measure inflationary pressures at the producer level and at the consumer level.

Bloomberg defines the producer price index (PPI) as follows:

> *Measures average changes in prices received by domestic producers of commodities in all stages of processing. When an establishment is selected to participate in the PPI survey, it is visited by a field economist who solicits the firm's voluntary cooperation and informs the firm of the strict confidentiality rules that will safeguard the information being requested. Once cooperation is obtained, the field economist uses the disaggregating technique to select the goods for which prices will be reported. From this point forward, the establishment reports prices for the selected products, usually on a monthly basis, on a form provided by the BLS. Most information used in calculating the indices is obtained through the systematic sampling of nearly every industry in the manufacturing and mining sectors of the economy. The PPI program also includes some information from other sectors—agriculture, fishing, forestry, services, and gas and electric. Producer price indices are designed to measure only the change in prices received for the output of domestic industries, therefore imports are not included. Each month approximately 100,000 prices are collected from 30,000 establishments.*

The consumer price index (CPI) is defined by Bloomberg as follows:

Represents changes in prices of all goods and services purchased for consumption by urban households. User fees (such as water and sewer service) and sales and excise taxes paid by the consumer are also included. Income taxes and investment items (i.e., stocks, bonds, and life insurance) are not included. CPI for urban consumers includes expenditures by urban wage earners and clerical workers, professional, managerial and technical workers, the self-employed, short-term workers, the unemployed, retirees and others not in the labor force. This represents about 80 percent of the total U.S. population.

The CPI and PPI, although both broad measures of inflationary pressures, paint a solid picture of current inflation levels. Because these indicators are so broad, both indexes capture the ongoing changing pricing pressures at both the consumer and producer levels. There may be little to no pressure as well, and this will be reflected by these reports. My view is that both indicators need to be looked at together. If looked at separately, they will provide solid data providing insight on the inflation front, but together, the complete inflation picture is provided.

Inflationary pressures also need to be looked at from a top-down approach. This is why it is important to use these reports in conjunction. Together the reports show data that start at the producer level that includes the cost of raw materials working all the way down to ultimately the end consumer. This approach and analysis should provide enough insight to make an educated assessment detailing whether there are rising prices at the producer level and if these price increases are able to be passed down to the consumer.

Common sense tells you that if there is an increase at the producer level, it should be passed through to and register at the consumer level. Truthfully, how often does common sense work the way it should when it comes to investing? Maybe 50 percent of the time? That number might be a little low. Whether it is 10 percent, 50 percent, or 75 percent, the economy and inflation signals at times defy common sense.

The bottom line is that you don't always see an increase in consumer prices when there is an uptick or increase at the producer level or vice versa. Just because the price of raw materials or the price of labor has increased doesn't mean that the producer is able to pass those costs on to the consumer. This is another example of why it is important to follow both indicators. Both tell a story individually, and when they are put together, a clearer picture emerges. Together, the two indexes might tell a slightly different story than they do individually.

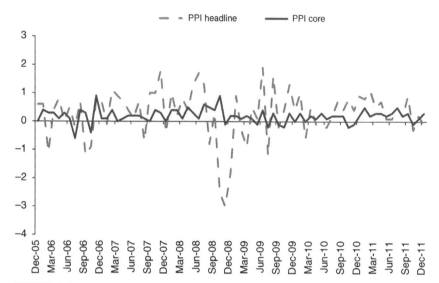

FIGURE 9.2 Represents the Relationship between Headline and Core Producer Price Index
Source: Bloomberg data.

Both the indicators are measured on a month-over-month increase and a year-over-year. Adding to the mix is another important piece to look at that excludes food and energy. This is known as the CPI ex Food and Energy and PPI ex Food and Energy. Food and energy are excluded because of the view that these categories have the tendency to skew the results in one direction or the other. This is due to the inherent volatility of both the food and energy sectors. Think about it this way: If there is a temporary spike in oil prices due to a weather-related event, the headline CPI (including food and energy) may show a significant jump for the month. The core number (excluding food and energy) attempts to reduce the volatility and reflect a more accurate read of trends.

I keep harping on trends. Why are they so important? Figures 9.2 and 9.3 show the monthly volatility of the PPI and CPI indexes.

You should be able to take away the importance of looking at longer-term trends and avoid getting caught up in the month-to month-numbers. Although the charts show some resemblance to one another, producers don't always have the luxury of passing higher costs through to the consumer. If the CPI is not reflecting the higher prices that the producers are feeling, who is absorbing the increase? That's right; the producer. If the higher costs do

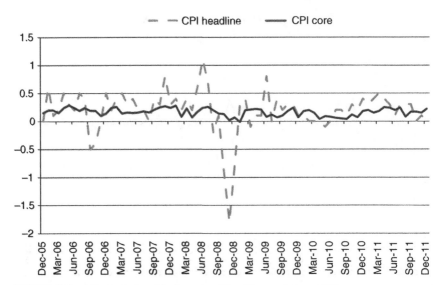

FIGURE 9.3 The Relationship between Headline and Core CPI
Source: Bloomberg data.

not normalize in a timely manner, the pricing pressures at this level will start to squeeze margins. As margins are squeezed, corporations will be forced to lower earnings expectations. What does that mean? And why should you care? Well, there are a number of reasons to be concerned and follow. For this discussion, you want to know that corporate guidance is being adjusted down, because it is the closest piece you have to a crystal ball. Forward-looking guidance will help telegraph the direction of corporate earnings and therefore ultimately impact the economy. Putting the pieces together is not always an easy task, and you may not always get it right. Either way, here is an example of how the economy, the Fed, inflation, and the markets can all work against each other.

The fourth quarter in 2008 tested investor common sense when it came to inflationary pressures and the Treasury Inflation Protected Securities (TIPS) market. At that time, equity markets were at the edge of a correction as the economy was in the thick of many tangled webs. Investors were trying to get their arms around the ramifications of the housing bubble and liquidity crisis, and preparing for what some most economists viewed as the worst recession since the Great Depression. What were the markets and economic indicators telling us? Economic growth was slowing and likely to continue down that path as consumers retreated and locked their wallets,

TABLE 9.2 Various Metrics to Measure Inflation

% Change	October	November	December	January
PPI MOM	−2.50%	−3.00%	−1.80%	0.90%
PPI YOY	5.20%	0.40%	−0.90%	−0.90%
PCE MOM	0.06%	0.03%	0.02%	0.10%
PCE YOY	2.20%	2.00%	1.80%	1.60%
CPI MOM	−0.90%	−1.80%	−0.80%	.030%
CPI YOY	3.70%	1.10%	0.10%	0.00%
Retail Sales	−3.90%	−3.10%	−2.60%	1.50%

Source: Bloomberg data.

allocating funds only to necessities. Table 9.2 shows the different tools to measure inflation. I compared both the month-over-month and year-over-year percent change headline CPI, PPI, and the U.S. Personal Consumption Expenditure Core Price index (PCE). The majority of the monthly data point to a decline or a deflationary threat brewing on the horizon. The headline CPI paints the most negative picture, with the entire fourth quarter in negative territory. As expected, the consumer turned cautious, as reflected by the retail sales data which averaged a negative 3.20 percent. With all the stars in alignment for the world to come crashing down, Treasury markets were off to the races and the threat of inflation discussed in prior quarters turned to the threat of deflation. Investors and consumers were reminded of the threat of deflation on an almost daily basis, as the phrase made its way into numerous headlines. The one piece of data in the table that did not project such a dire deflationary view was the PCE. Remember that this metric is the Fed's preferred tool for measuring inflation. The month-over-month numbers remained positive, as did the year-over-year numbers.

During the quarter, the Federal Open Market Committee (FOMC) also started aggressively adding accommodation. On October 8, 2008, the Fed stepped in, and at an unscheduled meeting, cut the overnight lending rate by 50 bps—to 1.5 percent—and lowered the discount rate by the same amount, to 1.75 percent. The Fed again stepped in on October 29, lowering the lending rate and the discount rate again by 50 bps to 1.00 percent and 1.25 percent, respectively. The committee wasn't even close to being finished. On December 16, 2008, as the outlook on economic growth continued to weaken, the Fed in a historic move lowered the fed funds target rate from 1 percent to a range of 0-25 bps—the level at which it stands as we move through 2012. If you combine the Fed activity and the data points from the PCE you have on your hands an FOMC that is willing to take market-friendly steps when it feels it is necessary to help support the economy.

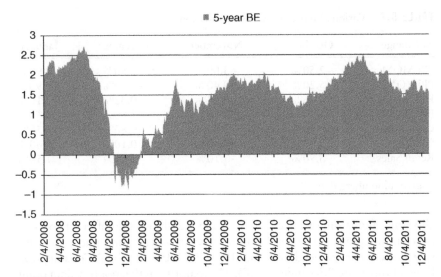

FIGURE 9.4   5-year break-even Rate
Source: Bloomberg data.

At your fingertips, you had an accommodative Fed and an inflation indicator that is preferred by the committee was pointing to benign, or even flat inflationary pressures. If that was the case, why were the inflation markets performing so poorly? Simply put, the markets were spooked and common sense was thrown out the window. The environment was tricky, with economists and others speaking about the potential threat of deflation. I just didn't see it materializing. Don't get me wrong, I did place a probability on a deflation event happening. I just placed a greater probability on the Fed taking the necessary steps and measures to keep that event from materializing.

Common sense told me that the market was pricing in too high a probability that inflation was turning to deflation, which is much harder to combat. Look closer at the TIPS market. Figure 9.4 represents the 5-year break-even rate.

The break-even rate is the difference between the yield of the TIP security and the nominal Treasury with a like maturity. It is also the expected inflation rate. The zero mark represents the crossover from inflation to deflation forecast by the break-even rate. Due to the aforementioned indicators and negative investor sentiment, the five-year inflation-protected security was trading at a negative break-even rate. Deflation was a serious concern within the sector. The problem was that the overconcern wasn't warranted at such levels. I have to admit I was not one who was initially buying on the way down. When the negative data started hitting the tape, I took a step back to look at the big picture and waited for the trends to develop. Once there was a string of positive monthly PCE prints—even when the CPI and retail sales data turned negative—I took a serious look at the current break-even levels, which were now over 100 bps lower, and decided it was time to go in. Purchasing TIPS when they were so far out of favor was the trade of the year. The purchases did not catch the bottom, but that was okay; they didn't have to. Once the data started turning positive the following month, deflation fears were calmed and positive inflation growth was back on the table. You may have heard it said before that the time to buy insurance is when you don't need it. The same idea holds true for investing. The TIPS sector had been shunned by investors for nearly three full months, and the time to buy was when almost nobody else wanted to purchase the sector. On my charts, the break-even rate hit a low on December 15, 2008, and widened approximately 136 bps before stabilizing. Remember, a widening break-even rate is positive if you are long the security.

CONSUMPTION: AMERICA'S FUEL

It is a well-known fact that the consumer is the backbone of the economy. Why is this? Consumer spending represents 70 percent of economic growth. There are different ways to measure consumer spending, but I feel that retail sales is a strong indicator that should not be overlooked.

Retail sales will help provide an early indication of what the future may bring. The data help provide guidance for the strength of the gross domestic product (GDP). Stronger numbers over time—for instance, quarter after quarter—indicate increased economic growth. One month, or even two months, of weak or strong data do not constitute a trend, and a trend is what you are looking for to help provide clarity on the economy. Weaker numbers may guide you to the conclusion that the economy is decelerating.

A very simple definition of a consumer is anyone who goes shopping and spends money that is contributing to the U.S. GDP. You are included in that category, as is your neighbor and anyone else who decides to open their wallet, whether it is to fill the gas tank or purchase a new computer. Consumers are what keep America going. There are multiple factors that could affect the spending habits of the consumer. Some spending trends are obvious and should not be too difficult to uncover. What happens to consumer habits when commodity prices increase? Consumers undoubtedly feel the pinch at the pump as the price of oil moves higher. Higher gas prices not only aggravate you, but also take some of the disposable cash out of your pocket. Most individuals would rather purchase a tangible item— maybe a new golf club, or dinner at a fancy restaurant—than buy gasoline for their car.

By monitoring the consumption data, you are able to get a good gauge on the health of the economy through the eyes of the consumer. If consumers are opening up their wallets, they are confident, which is a positive sign for economic growth. Successful analysis would take the next step and combine these data with the employment picture. If the consumers are confident with their jobs, they will be more willing to spend. To close this section, I will leave you with this thought: Consumer confidence fosters growth within the economy.

THE FEDERAL CHAIRMAN: THE WIZARD HIMSELF

The FOMC and its chairman are probably the most influential group when it comes to the fixed income markets. Because of this I have an entire chapter dedicated to the committee. It also deserves a place in the top indicators to watch. The problem: The FOMC is not an indicator and the committee meets approximately every six weeks. Even with a limited number of scheduled engagements, member comments are market moving. In addition to the committee's scheduled meetings, the chairman holds press conferences at least four times a year and committee members speak frequently at various venues. This transparency provides portfolio managers with the ammunition to try to get inside the committee's head, which at times can be dangerous. By doing so, the goal is to get the upper hand and insight on the direction of interest rates and the next, if any, policy move.

CHAPTER 10

The Yield Curve

You get recessions, you have stock market declines. If you don't understand that's going to happen, then you're not ready, you won't do well in the markets.

—Peter Lynch

The fixed income market has been on fire for a number of years. I leave it open for interpretation if you as an investor view that as a positive or a negative. In truth, it would depend on the time frame. It is easy to single out a particular year or set of years in which the market has rallied. On the other hand, there are multiple snapshots in time when, if you had entered into a long position and not held the position to maturity, the trade would have been a losing endeavor. Realizing that there is daily, monthly, and even yearly volatility, take a step back and look at the big picture over a longer time frame. The Treasury market specifically has shown a great run over the past few decades.

There's no denying that the Treasury sector is the recipient of the flight-to-quality trade, regardless of the driving force. Over the years, there has been chatter about other government debt markets potentially taking the safe haven role, replacing the U.S. Treasury market. To date, and looking into the foreseeable future, this doesn't seem to be in the cards. It can't go without notice that over time there are moves higher and lower in price reacting to the current headlines, which at that point in time, are the be-all and end-all. However the market is sliced and diced, over the long term, we have seen a strong bull market since the early 1980s. In late September 1981, the 10-year Treasury was yielding approximately 15.84 percent. From there, it was all downhill, finishing—or possibly, just pausing—at 1.87 percent on December 30, 2011. Figure 10.1 shows the massive rally witnessed over the decades; only time will tell if the run is over or not.

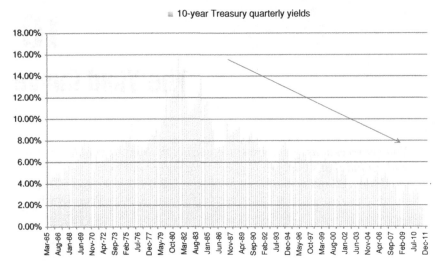

FIGURE 10.1 10-year Quarterly yields
Source: Bloomberg data.

With such a strong move pushing yields to these historic low levels, it is inevitable that there will be a reversal of fortune. Eventually, the tides will turn. Interest rates represented by the Treasury sector will move higher, pushing prices lower. It is not a question of if it is going to happen, but when it will happen. There were multiple factors that drove prices up and pushed yields to these absolute levels. Whether fundamentals are depressing interest rates or they are artificially held low by central bank activity, in the end, it really doesn't matter. The plain fact is that the move occurred. What does it mean, and how does it affect the Treasury yield curve?

As with any market or sector, there are unique characteristics that impact fixed income portfolios. Most of these characteristics are distinctive and may have little direct bearing on other fixed income asset classes. The unique characteristics are not represented by just one type of strategy or security type. They are also not driven by the style of the manager or the strategy he or she implements—passive or active, long or short, the impact from the yield curve is very similar. What differs is how it impacts the strategy. First let's take a look at three risks that are inherent to almost all bond portfolios and their relationship to the yield curve.

1. Interest rate risk
2. Default risk
3. Reinvestment risk

These risks are found in almost every type of fixed income portfolio. The same risks are found within a Treasury-only or government portfolio, though in a slightly different order.

1. Interest rate risk
2. Reinvestment risk
3. Default risk

Why a different order? Default risk should be minimal unless you have a bleak outlook on the state of the U.S. government. Don't laugh—or maybe we should pause and take a moment to laugh. The unthinkable act of a U.S. government default carriess a low probability, but it has recently started to increase. History has shown multiple occurrences when the U.S. government has in one fashion or another defaulted or come very close. The most recent event took place back in August 2011, when there was a showdown around raising the debt ceiling. This created the fear that a default or missed coupon payment, ultimately leading to a downgrade of the United States' coveted triple-A rating by a top rating agency.

Before we move on, let's define these three risks.

1. **Interest rate risk**—How the portfolio is affected by the movement of interest rates.
2. **Reinvestment risk**—The risk that a bond with a specific coupon is able to be reinvested at a similar rate to that at which it was purchased within the current interest rate environment. There is greater risk of not capturing, or finding it hard to replicate, similar bond characteristics when interest rates are falling or rallying. This is due to the inverse relationship between prices and yields.
3. **Default risk**—The most straight forward of the three. It is the risk that your coupon payments or principal will not be repaid to you on the expected dates or at maturity.

Let's start with the good news—and there is always a way to put a positive spin on the situation. The good news is that as an investor, you have the ability to mitigate these risks. One way to attempt this is to understand how the yield curve affects your portfolio and what its movements or shape are telling you.

The yield curve is a snapshot in time of specific bond yields shown spanning across different maturities. Different investors may define the yield curve differently as they refer to various segments or points represented

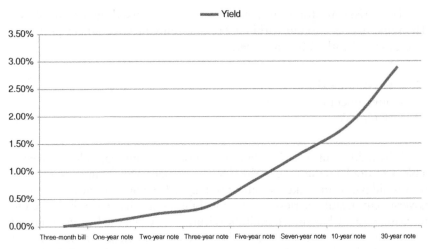

FIGURE 10.2 Treasury Curve
Source: Bloomberg data.

by a set of bond maturities. For example, a money market yield curve is
represented by securities from overnight to those with a final maturity of
13 months. This curve has its own metrics and nuances, which are fundamentally and technically different. It exists unilaterally, or in combination
with agency discount notes, U.S. T-bills, commercial paper, or even lending metrics such as LIBOR. When a yield curve is discussed, investors are
usually referring to the Treasury curve. The yield curve terminology is not
analogous to just the Treasury sector. When trading corporate securities, the
credit curve is utilized. Credit spreads, which make up the curve or spread
curve, are the difference between the yield of a corporate security and the
Treasury yield. This spread is plotted in a similar manner, painting a story
for investors about the credit market. The terminology of the two is slightly
different. but the information gleaned is similar, and a is necessity when it
comes to investing. When you hear or read about the credit curve, this is
what is being discussed.

The most talked-about curve is the U.S. Treasury curve, which usually
refers to the three-month bill through the 30-year bond, with varying points
in between. Figure 10.2 represents the most widely looked-at points along
the curve when assessing the broad interest rates market.

It is common to find bonds with longer maturities having a higher
yield, unless there is some type of optionality structured into the bond.
Optionality is usually not infused into the Treasury market. One caveat
on the horizon: the U.S. government is discussing the possibility of issuing

a floating rate note Treasury security. Details are not finalized about this security, but if issuance of a floating rate note Treasury becomes reality, it will be a unique offering within the sector. Optionality is found more frequently within the government agency sector through the issuance of callable securities, mortgages, and securities where there are floating rate coupons.

The larger coupon for longer-dated maturities is straightforward. Ask yourself the question, don't I deserve to earn more interest when I lend my money to the issuer—the government, for instance—for a longer time? Hopefully, your answer is also yes. I would expect to receive a higher return if I lend the government money for 30 years versus for two years. Due to those common sense parameters, longer-dated bonds should always have a greater yield than those with shorter maturities. That doesn't mean they always do.

THE SPREAD

A common way to analyze the yield curve is to calculate the spread. The spread is quoted by taking the difference, or spread, between two points. This calculation can be made at any segment of the curve. The most common example that is quoted is the relationship between the 2-year yield and the 10-year yield. Although the spread between the 2-year yield and 10-year yield is the most commonly quoted, the spread or relationship between two securities can be studied on any securities. This analysis helps uncover the dislocations that in the end present opportunities.

Figure 10.3 reflects the movement of the 2-year, 10-year spread over 2011. Over the course of the year, the spread steadily declined, moving lower—narrowing—by 106 basis points (bps) from the end of 2010 to the end of 2011. On December 31, 2010, the spread held at 269 bps. Remember, this is the difference in yield between the 2-year and 10-year Treasury notes. This spread is what investors required at the time to add duration and invest further out the yield curve. One year later, on December 30, 2011, investors demanded less yield pickup to extend eight years out the curve. At this point, the spread was reduced to 163 bps. The change in heart was driven by multiple factors. The uncertainties within the global economy and European default concerns were unending. In addition, the Federal Open Market Committee (FOMC) was in the midst of rebalancing its current balance sheet holdings and laying the groundwork for interest rates to remain low for an extended period of time. If we break down the spread a little further for the year, it is clearly visible in Figure 10.4 that the 10-year yield fell further and at a more rapid pace than the 2-year note. This flattening

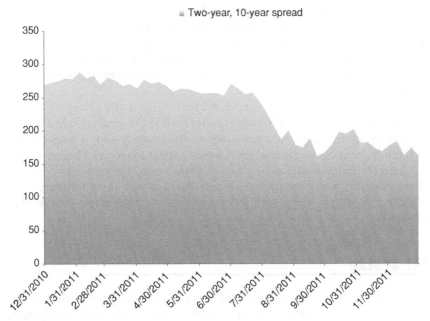

FIGURE 10.3 Two-year, 10-year spread
Source: Bloomberg data.

bias was expected, taking shape in a bull flattener fashion; that is, the longer maturity outperforms the shorter maturity. The aforementioned events and the low yields artificially created by the Fed pushed investors out the yield curve, amplifying this move.

THE MONEY MARKET ARENA

Let's revisit the money market sector. Money market portfolio managers investing in the money market arena are not too concerned with the 2-year, 10-year spread, because it does not directly impact or drive their investing decisions. Successful investing within the money market sector is driven by daily decisions made about where to place money along the money market curve. A standard representation of the money market curve is those securities with maturities between overnight and 13 months. The pickup in yield is usually much smaller across the curve within the world of money market investing. There are anomalies similar to other sectors. Unfortunately, the anomalies that create dislocations within the front end are usually not found

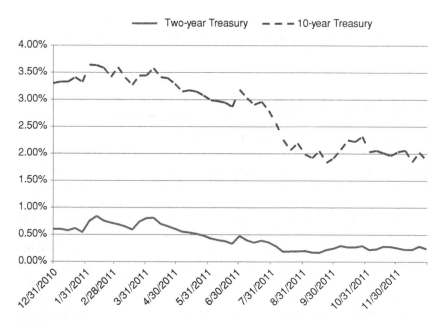

FIGURE 10.4 Two- year and 10-year
Source: Bloomberg data.

very attractive to the front-end investor. Increased yield is usually a trade-off for increased risk. A money market fund or strategy designed with the preservation of capital in mind isn't comfortable with taking on additional risk.

Short-term investors are able to benefit by investing out the curve. Picking and choosing your spots will help drive performance. Excluding security selection, the yield curve is a primary driver for returns. Every day, a similar food fight takes place in the search for an extra basis point. The statement "the early bird catches the worm" truly comes into play. Individuals who arrive first in the office have the greatest selection and investing options. This is one reason why money market managers are usually fixated on the computer screens at their desk no later than 7:00 A.M., ready to start trading for the day. Adding to the pressure is the low interest rate environment and the ongoing theme of at times, unlimited risk. This is why every basis point counts. The difference between an overnight security yielding 10 bps and 12 bps doesn't seem like a huge deal, but the 2 bps may help set you apart. On the other hand, when they do the math, the outright yield level can be disheartening to an outside observer, and the additional pickup is negligible. For instance, if you are investing $50 million overnight at 10 bps, you would earn roughly $139. The additional pickup of two bps adds $27 to the overnight return. Not too exciting, but still $27 more than you had the prior day. Unfortunately, that is the environment the front-end investor must navigate, day in and day out.

THE DIRECTION OF RATES

A normal yield curve is represented by longer-dated bonds carrying a higher yield. Although classified as normal, this relationship is not always present. There are different times and environments when the yield on the long bond—that is, a bond with 30 years before it matures—has a similar or lower yield than that of a two-year. As discussed earlier, the shape of the yield curve will help you dictate the direction not only of interest rates, but the economy too. How can this be? Why are interest rates so important? What is the first question you ask your mortgage broker when you are looking to buy a house or your sales agent when looking to finance a car? "What is the interest rate?" That is pretty straightforward. With high probability, the lower the rate is, the more likely it is that you move forward with the purchase. When in discussions with their mortgage brokers and close to locking in your mortgage rate, most individuals will try to asses the economy or at least themselves whether they think rates will move higher or lower from here. How do you know with certainty that you are at the bottom of an interest rate or economic cycle? You don't. It is important to try to assess the situation. Similar activity should take place in your fixed income portfolio. The question is, where do you start in this assessment? One option you have is to start with the yield curve. The yield curve is utilized by economists and asset managers every day to assess the direction of the economy. The shape of the curve helps predict future economic activity. In order to assess the economy from the shape of the yield curve, we need to take a look at the different shapes and what they mean.

There are four common shapes the yield curve could form. They are

1. Normal
2. Steep
3. Flat
4. Inverted

The normal yield curve is an upward sloping curve, as was discussed previously. As you work your way out the curve, longer-dated bonds carry a reasonably higher yield than the previous point on the curve. Figure 10.5 shows the Treasury yield curve on December 30, 2011. You can see that the

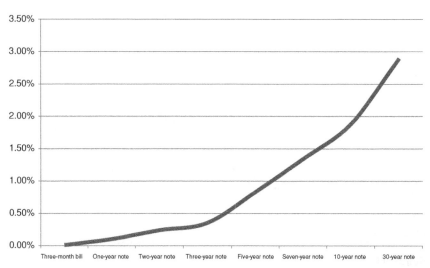

FIGURE 10.5 Positive yield curve
Source: Bloomberg data.

shape of the curve is gradually moving higher. The 2-year, 10-year spread is 164 bps.

A STEEP YIELD CURVE

A steep yield curve is represented when the difference or spread between two points on the curve is abnormally wide. For example, as shown in Figure 10.6, the 2 -year, 10-year spread at the end of 2011 was 164 bps. Rewind to the end of 2009 and the two-year, 10-year spread was 270 bps. Obviously, the 270 basis points is a greater number, therefore a steeper curve. You can see this in Figure 10.6, which overlays the 2-year, 10-year spread on December 31, 2009, and the yield curve in 2011. You can see that the top line is increasing at a steeper angle between the 2- and 10-year points than the dashed line.

One way the yield curve steepens is by the 10-year selling off at a faster pace than the 2-year. This action will create a wider spread or gap between the two points on the curve.

The spread that used to be 270 bps in 2009 finished 2011 at 164 bps. In this example, the 2-year, 10-year curve was steeper by 106 bps in 2009. Usually, a steeper yield curve is tied to an economy with a loose or easy monetary policy. Throughout 2009, the economy was on shaky ground and

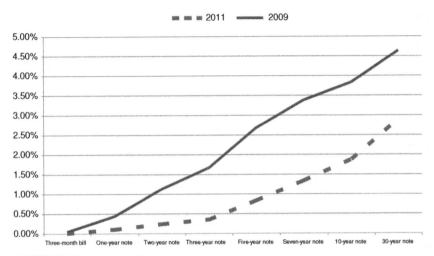

FIGURE 10.6 Steep yield curves
Source: Bloomberg data.

the Federal Reserve was pumping cash into the system in efforts to generate economic growth. Remember back to the section that addressed the FOMC. A loose monetary policy is initiated in an attempt to spur growth within the economy. The typical bond market reaction would be for the longer end of the yield curve—represented by the 10- through 30-year—to underperform the rest of the yield curve. This underperformance may be attributable to the threat of future inflationary pressures. Another way to phrase this is that the yield of the 10-year note will rise faster than the rest of the curve. Remember, when yields rise, prices fall. If the yield is rising at a faster pace than the other points on the curve, prices are falling at a more rapid pace.

A FLAT YIELD CURVE

As we just covered, a steep yield curve is represented when the spread between two points on the curve is wide and likely to widen further. When discussing the yield curve with a flatter bias or shape, similarities with a steep curve are present. The main difference, which you can glean from the name, is the actual shape that the yields represent when plotted. Figure 10.7 shows that the line representing the curve is becoming more flat or a straight line when plotted.

The curve receives its shape—and its name—from the yields from either the long end or the front end converging on each other. The flattening shape

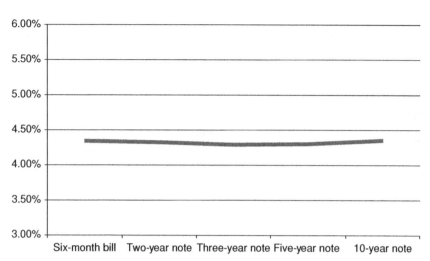

FIGURE 10.7 Flat yield curve
Source: Bloomberg data.

could start with the long end rallying more than the front end of the curve, which is known as a bull flattener. A bear flattener is when the front end of the curve starts selling off quicker than the long end. The front end may sell off as investors start pricing in upcoming Fed activity. For example, one scenario when the curve could take this shape is when the economy is overheating and the Federal Reserve is trying to put the brakes on growth. When the long end rallies, the view might be that inflation is expected to recede, or at the very least, hold constant, and the market will price this in pushing the long end lower. The most common and notable impetus for the curve to flatten is the flight-to-quality bid. When there is uncertainty in the markets or world economy, investors flock to the Treasury market, pushing prices higher. This move could be witnessed in parallel fashion—that is, the entire curve receives the bid, and therefore, the entire line shifts lower—but that would not represent a flattening yield curve. Real money buyers, hedge funds, corporate pensions, and insurance companies flock to the 10-year point on the curve as a normal trade that occurs in a flight-to-quality move.

AN INVERTED YIELD CURVE

Last in the lineup of yield curve shapes is the sometimes-feared inverted yield curve. An inverted curve is when the long end of the yield curve carries a

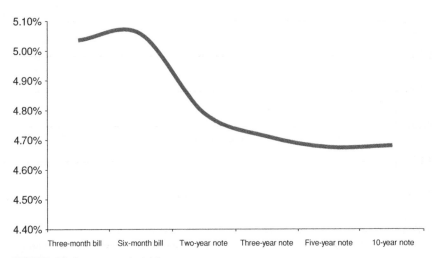

FIGURE 10.8 Inverted yield curve
Source: Bloomberg data.

yield that is lower than the two-year or front end of the curve. The long
end is usually represented by the 10-year or 30-year points on the curve.
Figure 10.8 clearly shows the negative spread between the front end of the
yield curve and the longer end. The spread at the turn of the year between
the 3-month Treasury bill and the 10-year Treasury note is negative 35 bps.
That is the difference between the 10-year that was yielding 4.68 percent,
and 5.036 percent on the three-month Treasury bill.

So what does this really mean? This shape of the curve is heavily debated.
The question that frequently arises, particularly in a shift of the curve, is
whether an inverted yield curve signals troubled times ahead for the economy. Some investors would answer without hesitating with a definitive yes.
Others might not, citing different factors that may influence the market, creating the inversion. Of course, these differences in opinion are what make a
market. If history holds any merit and weight, the answer is yes. Although
not always, an inverted yield curve typically precedes an environment of
slowing economic growth.

Figure 10.8 is telegraphing the economic environment back at the start
of 2007. Think back to the mid- to late 2006 time frame, and how the
economic environment was on the cusp of transforming, shifting gears. The
FOMC completed its current tightening campaign, pausing and holding
the fed funds rate at 5.25 percent after the June 29 meeting. This pause
occurred approximately three months after Ben Bernanke took the position
of chairman. The current policy concern was the risk of inflation. The

housing market was starting to show signs of slowing after a historic run. This housing slowdown will ultimately reduce the amount of borrowing and cash that is in circulation. It is common for a slowdown in housing to weigh heavily on economic growth. The Fed was pausing from removing accommodation, which this time, coincided as a signal of slowing growth. The word "recession" did not yet formally make its way into the daily vocabulary, though. It did, however, from time to time arise when discussions were had about the yield curve and future action from the Fed, investors, and the economy. Many investors and economists who challenged or were against the talk of recession signaled that rates were low and the curve inverted for various reasons. One reason was the increased demand. Where does the type of demand come from to artificially lower the long end of the yield curve enough to invert the curve? At the time, China was a strong buyer of U.S. debt. Adding fuel to the fire was the elevated price in oil. Profits generated from oil-producing countries had to be placed somewhere; why not the U.S. Treasury market? In 2011 and 2012, large buyers of Treasury securities are the central banks from around the world. The FOMC specifically influenced the buying patterns.

You can see how there were outside influences—such as central bank activity—that inevitably and realistically can drive yields lower. The Fed was on the sidelines and holding firm with its current policy. As we turned the corner into the new year, the economic landscape was solid, excluding the housing market. Looking back, it was obviously a large exclusion, and if it had been handled properly, a significant amount of pain would have been avoided. The long end of the yield curve was influenced by heavy buying. If only investors had subscribed to—and maybe you did—and followed along with the notion that an inverted yield curve signals a future slowdown, they would have had the right trade in play. The activity from the FOMC signaled to the market that inflation was not, or should not, be a terrible concern. As time rolled on, events such as the housing bubble popping played out. Ultimately, this played a role in the collapse of the financial system and confirmed the view that inflation was not likely to come into play.

LISTEN TO THE CURVE

In the end, you need to respect the yield curve. At times, it may be difficult to peel back the onion or block out all—or at least some—of the outside occurrences and see the light. When you are able to achieve this, you will see that the yield curve is a tool that will provide insight to help gauge economic growth and the future direction of interest rates. There are so many different pieces or silos of information that can, and will, influence the shape of the yield curve. It is understandable that it can be daunting. All of the aforementioned categories and examples paint a picture of four different and unique scenarios that impact and influence investment strategy and economic conditions. These are clear examples of how interest rates and the economy are very much linked to one another.

CHAPTER 11

The Ladder and Why You Need One

Only buy something that you'd be perfectly happy to hold if the market shut down for 10 years.

—Warren Buffett

Fixed income markets tend to carry the reputation of being very complex. This is accurate in some cases; however, it doesn't have to be. Truth be told, investing in fixed income markets is as complex as you want it to be. This is true in every sense imaginable. Investors have the tendency to get caught up in the details and complexities of the bond market. This mind-set is driven by all the different investment types and vehicles. If you let yourself fall into the trap, you will see that it is very easy to be pulled further into the complexities and find yourself inundated with Greek letters. This is, of course, only if you let yourself. It is easier than you think to get pulled in, and why not? All you have to do is turn on a business channel or pick up the financial paper and you are sure to read an article on mortgage securities, currencies, or structured debt. The times have definitely changed. There are many strategies that may hold complex characteristics. These complex strategies may be very rewarding, but as with anything, the greater the potential for reward, the greater the chance is for risk.

A successful fixed income strategy doesn't have to be complex; just well-constructed. Leave your risk taking to other asset classes where risk is well rewarded. Taking risk in an equity fund or hedge fund is likely to be much more fruitful than the return of a bond fund.

Whether embarking on a new strategy, balanced with other asset classes, or working with only fixed income securities, a sound strategy is very important. Regardless of how the portfolio will eventually be structured, a fixed income component is an integral part of your investment strategy. This strategy is applicable in varying degrees, whether you are an advisor, generalist portfolio manager, or an asset manager who specializes in a specific sector. You should know common terminology such as duration, coupon, yield, and call date like the back of your hand. Convexity, skewness and kurtosis, and paydown have a tendency to be viewed as more complex concepts, because understanding and successfully applying them is challenging even for the most seasoned asset manager. It is important not to get overwhelmed, to get back to basics and implement a solid and successful fixed income strategy.

There are many different strategies that are viable within the fixed income market. The end investor or portfolio guidelines will determine which strategy is the best fit. A straightforward strategy that I find very successful, particularly if you are in the distribution phase of investing, is a low-turnover strategy called a bond ladder. A laddered bond strategy is one of the most straightforward fixed income strategies and easiest to understand and feel confident about. Simple or straightforward does not mean ineffective, though. Over time, a well-executed and maintained bond ladder is, in my opinion, one of the most successful low-volatility fixed income strategies.

There are many benefits to the laddered bond strategy, which I will dive into later in this chapter. This strategy is not constrained to a particular sector or asset class. It can be implemented using multiple sectors that include municipals, government corporate securities, or any combination thereof. The strategy is also not limited to these sectors; I just view them as the most popular.

HOW IT WORKS

A laddered bond strategy involves evenly investing a portfolio of bonds in different maturities, sometimes referred to as buckets. This occurs over a set time frame. The concept should be easy for an investor to understand. The key principle of the strategy is that there need to be maturities in each year of the ladder. Is this a hard and fast rule? Not necessarily, but an evenly distributed ladder works best for the strategy to accomplish its stated goals. These goals will be discussed later in this chapter.

The Concept

When a bond matures, the proceeds are invested in a bond in the subsequent year of the strategy. This is known as investing in the next rung of the ladder. Let's walk through an example of a how a five-year laddered

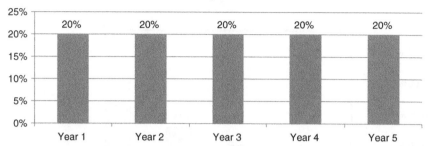

FIGURE 11.1 A Well-Constructed Ladder Investing in Equal Percentage Weights over the Term of the Ladder

bond strategy would be constructed. For this example, assume you have a portfolio of $100,000 to invest. We know the amount to invest, and we know the time frame to invest, which is five years. Now let me demonstrate how straightforward the concept really is. What needs to happen is an even investment of the available cash across the five years. In a five-year strategy, that would mean investing 20 percent of the portfolio in each year, since dividing 100 percent by 5 gives you 20 percent. If it is a 10-year ladder, a similar calculation occurs; in that example, 100 percent is divided by 10 to get a 10 percent allocation, which is then invested accordingly across the strategy horizon. Figure 11.1 represents a five-year ladder from a percentage viewpoint and what it would look like invested. If invested properly, each year has an equal weight of investments or maturities, or sometimes a combination of both. You can see how the years invested look like the rungs of a ladder. A sideways ladder, but a ladder nonetheless. Figure 11.2 shows the same ladder, with the incremental yield pickup represented across each rung. In a normal yield curve environment, the further out you extend the yield curve, the greater the yield. Figure 11.2 also depicts how the ladder process works. When the highlighted bond in Year 1 matures, it is reinvested out to the next rung of the ladder. In this example, that would be Year 5. Figure 11.3 shows an uneven ladder and how the cash flows and maturities would not be even.

You can see that Year 2 and Year 3 are underinvested. Although this is not detrimental, it does depict how uneven the maturities would run. Less maturities each year creates two possible problems. First, an unevenly invested ladder provides less of an ability for a manager to attempt to reduce the portfolio's interest rate risk. It also creates inconsistent yearly cash flows. Remember, reducing interest rate risk is accomplished by reinvesting

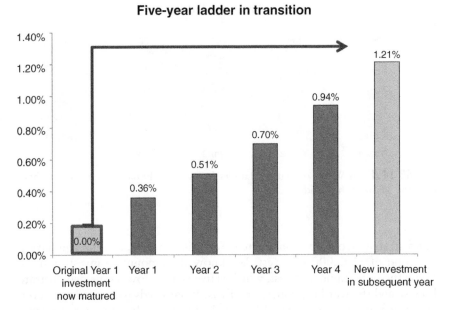

FIGURE 11.2 A Ladder in Transition with Represented Yields

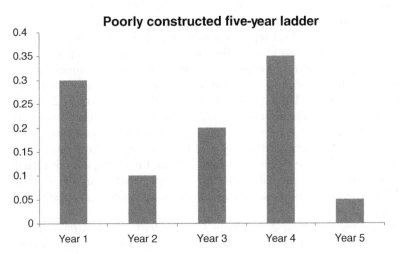

FIGURE 11.3 A Poorly Constructed Laddered Strategy Shown by the Uneven Weights

maturing bonds in the last leg of the ladder at the current market interest rates.

The structure of a laddered strategy naturally helps to insulate the portfolio from adverse or unfavorable market conditions. The goal of a laddered strategy is to provide, over time, suitable performance in any interest rate environment and markets. The goal relating to its construction is to invest in bonds that can handle the test of time. That means no high-flyers. What do I mean by this? When you are looking for suitable bonds to build out your strategy, don't just buy the cheapest bond on the block. Buying out-of-favor bonds for the wrong reason is asking for trouble. For example, it is very easy to find yourself investing in non-U.S. banks. To start, supply within this sector is a spigot that can't be turned off. The recent yield advantage will also test your discipline. If you feel that you are being pulled into this trap, take a step back and ask yourself, should my portfolio be heavily concentrated in the financial sector? A heavy concentration could be detrimental due to ongoing risks from the financial institution's balance sheet. Additionally, the noise from headline news that resurfaces from time to time has the ability to disrupt the structure of the ladder, resulting in potential losses if a company falls on difficult times. Many European financial institutions are trading at a discount to financial institutions within the United States and other countries. Ultimately, you need to take a disciplined approach, keeping close to your heart how quickly trouble can arise. Even in the good times, you need to acknowledge that a portfolio full of bank names is not a well-diversified portfolio.

The Goal

An investor may implement a bond ladder if he or she is seeking consistent results that may be generated in different interest rate environments. To elaborate, the strategy will do well in a bull market, which is when prices are rising and yields falling. Over time, it should also do well in a bear market, when prices are falling and yields are rising. The added benefit of this strategy is that it is designed to hold up well in a range-bound market as well. Performance should be defined—in all previous examples, and for the rest of the chapter—as preservation of capital and the ability to receive consistent current income. Key to achieving solid performance is to avoid defaults or bonds that have a deteriorating credit profile. High-quality bonds are purchased with the view that all coupons are to be made and the company's balance sheet is strong enough to minimize the odds against ratings action. Remember, in the end, for a low-turnover strategy, ratings actions will create volatility. Volatility will not impact the end result if the bonds are held to maturity and you receive the repayment of your funds.

Navigating through the ins and outs of markets is challenging, to say the least. Market gyrations, even if expected, can be daunting. And let's be honest, it is very difficult to consistently predict market moves, even for professionals. The best fund manager misses the mark from time to time. Let's face it, we are all human. The trick is to get more right than wrong. The beauty of a ladder strategy is that the goal of a laddered portfolio is straightforward. Straightforwardness with transparency is welcome after the chain of events that occurred within the markets beginning in the summer of 2007. The events that occurred could not have been scripted any better. The asset backed commercial paper (ABCP) and structured investment vehicles (SIV) came under pressure near the beginning of the trauma, which started the ball rolling. Following that, the straw that broke the camel's back was the "too big to fail" dilemma within the financial sector in 2008 and the start of the global recovery in 2009. Remember, it didn't stop there. The U.S. economy showed signs of strengthening; however, global economies started to come under pressure. Debt burdens across the globe started to impact financial markets, affecting investors. Uncertainty fell across various regions, from Ireland to the Middle East, finally settling within the eurozone. With the recent turn of events, it is easy to say that all markets, not only the fixed income market, have been challenging. After the headaches and turbulence of recent years, I have found that investors are eager to implement a strategy that has straightforward goals and will provide a benefit them in almost any period. At this point, the direction of interest rates, although a concern, is not at the top of everyone's list.

Look at the strategy from a different angle. Investments are made within the strategy that simply and clearly help mitigate interest rate risk. How does that work? If interest rates move higher, the portfolio will perform well within that interest rate environment. Why is that? Remember, as bonds mature, the proceeds are invested in the next rung or year of the ladder. If interest rates are moving higher in a bear market, the bonds that are maturing have a lower yield than the bonds that will be purchased. If a bond maturing was purchased at par yielding 2 percent and paying a coupon of 2 percent, it is providing $200 a year for every $10,000 invested. If the maturing bond is replaced with a bond yielding 3 percent and paying a coupon of 3 percent, not only is the average coupon of the portfolio going to increase, but you just increased your income by 1 percent, or $100 a year. That is pretty straightforward.

A similar scenario occurs in a bull market environment. If interest rates are rallying, you find your investment portfolio is in the midst of a bull market. This might be a time when volatility is increased. Volatility or not, the fixed income market does not stop. Usually, in this environment, it just so happens that you have a bond maturing. Even a rallying market is a positive for a portfolio with maturing bonds. In a bull market, the yields on your securities will move lower as the price of the bonds moves higher. In this scenario, your fixed income positions are appreciating as prices move higher. The downside is that you are replacing a maturing bond with one that may have a lower yield and coupon. The positive is that there will likely be a significant amount of supply. Companies always like to issue in a bull market. The nature of the strategy helps to mitigate this risk in this market as well. The maturing bond is replaced with another bond, which is placed in the next rung of the ladder. In a five-year strategy, the maturing bond is replaced with a bond that has a five-year maturity. This helps mitigate reinvestment risk because the bond with the longer maturity usually carries a higher yield than the maturing bond.

A benefit of a well-constructed laddered bond strategy is that it satisfies income needs while preserving capital. This strategy provides investors the ability to forecast and receive income from a fixed coupon payment. Due to these characteristics, there are many reasons that an investor may look to implement this strategy. It is a popular strategy where the portfolio is geared for consistent distributions. That is, the portfolio will be managed for income with a set amount of funds. The asset manager should not expect the ongoing addition of new funds. In addition, a primary reason to implement this strategy is the preservation of capital.

To a fixed income investor, preservation of capital is usually one of the most important characteristics. A laddered bond strategy accomplishes this in a number of different ways. First, the portfolio has minimal turnover. Portfolio turnover is a term that is used frequently within the equity market and when discussing certain fixed income bond funds. Turnover is exactly what it sounds like: the percentage of the holdings within the portfolio that is turned over. Another way to look at this is how frequently the manager of the fund or separate account buys and sells securities. There should be little turnover within a laddered bond strategy. The lack of turnover does not burden the portfolio with realized gains or losses—losses that could inadvertently reduce the portfolio value, not to mention create additional tax measures on the investor.

THE LONG END POSES CHALLENGES

I will say it right up front: The long end of the yield curve should be left alone unless you have specific and unique goals. Before we go any further, let's define the long end. This is the part of the curve that represents 20- to 30-year maturities. Primarily, institutional investors utilize this part of the curve. These investors are who you would think they are; for example, corporations and pension funds. Institutional investors have a completely different investment goal. They are usually not looking for current income derived from a coupon stream. These investors are utilizing the long end for different strategies. For example, institutional investors may utilize the long end of the curve to match liabilities through various strategies, one known as LDI or liability driven investing.

The long end of the yield curve is known for market volatility. Market volatility leads to portfolio volatility. Volatility is usually a negative characteristic for an investor who is seeking income or concerned about the potential for realized or even unrealized losses. Some investors, institutional or otherwise, may not want to worry about having to time a redemption in a volatile market. A few examples might be an education expense or an unexpected capital outlay. Why put yourself in the situation where you may be forced to take a loss holding a high-quality bond just because of market volatility?

Here lies the problem. The 20- and 30-year part of the yield curve may be enticing to investors in a low-turnover strategy. One reason is that additional supply goes hand in hand with that particular part of the curve. Depending on the interest rate cycle, the long end of the yield curve may be very favorable for companies to issue debt in. Low interest rates equal cheap long-term funding for corporations. It makes sense that a company would term out its debt; that is, retire current debt at the front end of the curve and reissue it for 30 years at low yields. Therefore, depending on the cycle, there may be ample supply in this part of the yield curve. We saw this happen when the fed funds rate was held in the range of 0 to 25 basis points. The other alluring characteristic of the long end of the curve is that bonds with longer maturities usually carry an increased yield and potentially larger coupons. This is very enticing to some investors, particularly if they are looking to achieve a certain coupon to provide a specified amount of income from the portfolio. Duration, a concept we all know well, is another characteristic that usually increases as a bond moves out the yield curve. This trait is not as appealing to those accounts in a low-turnover strategy or that subscribe to the notion that volatility may be negative. Unless the bond has specific optionality or unique characteristics, the longer the bond, the greater the duration the bond carries. A bond that has a longer duration is impacted more by changes to interest rate movement. This increased duration could create an increase in general market volatility and an increase in the price volatility of a bond. The extra yield that you may pick up, and I did say yes you may pick up, is not worth the extra risk that is attached to the bond. I am sure you have heard before that there is no such thing as free ride; this holds true within the fixed income market as well. Investors have learned over the years, particularly since the Great Recession, that when something looks too good to be true, it probably is.

For example, if bond (A) has a higher yield than bond (B), but both have similar maturities and credit ratings, the bonds are not truly similar. Take a hard look at the characteristics of each bond. The additional yield you are receiving is likely indicating that the credit profile or liquidity characteristics between the two bonds are different.

The Front End Is Technical

When discussing the yield curve or credit curve, let me first clarify what I determine to be the front end. For the purpose of discussing appropriate terms for ladder strategies, the front end of the yield curve is the spread between overnight securities and those with a final stated maturity of 13 months. This particular section of the curve is very unique. It trades unlike like other sectors within the fixed income market. Excluding the financial companies, such as banks, insurers, and broker dealers, issuance is secondary to most companies. From my experience, financial institutions represent approximately 60 percent of issuance within the very front end of the credit curve. Because so much supply comes from the financial sector, it is, at times, very challenging to remain diversified. It isn't always this way, though more often than not, it seems to be.

The front end is like the bastard child of the fixed income market. Excluding government securities, it is also essentially viewed as second-best by the issuing community. Why are banks so involved in the front end? They need overnight funding to maintain and run their business.

Varieties of Short-Term Strategies

There are passive strategies that are created in an effort to provide an enhanced yield to a money market strategy. There are also different active strategies that aim to take advantage of the dislocations within the money market and short-term arena. These strategies have different risks that are always fully uncovered through different market cycles. They are not always present, but have a tendency to rear their ugly heads when investing in this type of strategy. There are significant differences between these cash alternative strategies and a laddered strategy. Most of these strategies require a more active approach. A key difference is that the active mandate will have a higher turnover ratio, which may generate both realized gains and losses. As discussed earlier, the turnover ratio is how many times the bonds are changed within the portfolio. A laddered strategy, even with a low turnover ratio, is also able to take advantage of certain dislocations within the front end of the credit and yield curve.

You do give up yield by investing within the front end of the curve, which hinders your creation of annual income. Unless you are designing your strategy with a short-term goal in mind, it may make more sense to incorporate the front end of the yield curve within a longer-dated strategy. In other words, leave the front end alone unless you are creating a strategy designed to replace a money market strategy or the front end is a compliment to a longer-dated strategy.

THE SWEET SPOT

Okay, so if I am telling you to avoid securities that reside within the first 13 months in the yield curve, the front end, and I am also stating to avoid the long end or the 20- to 30-year portion of the curve, than what is left? The sweet spot is the place to be. What is the sweet spot? The sweet spot is what I refer to as the belly of the yield curve. The term "belly of the curve" is sometimes thrown around representing different time periods or buckets. The six- to 12-year time frame within the yield curve is usually viewed as the belly, but some investors may narrow this range to the eight- to 10-year frame, and others may expand it. For building a ladder, I make a minor modification when defining the belly of the curve, stretching the range by three years. By stretching the range to include the 3-year to 10-year points or buckets, you have now created the sweet spot. From a pure market perspective, this range contains the optimal years to use when creating a ladder strategy. Let me be clear that ladder strategies can be utilized throughout other maturity buckets. Investors have different needs and goals, which may present the need to structure a strategy outside the sweet spot, which makes complete sense. But the sweet spot carries true beneficial characteristics. There are three characteristics that are represented in the sweet spot: liquidity, consistent coupons, and ample supply.

LIQUIDITY

If you ask five individuals to define liquidity, you will likely receive three to five different definitions. There are a handful of ways to describe liquidity. Although you may receive five different answers for the definition of liquidity, there is only one correct answer.

Liquidity does not just represent the ability to be able to buy and sell bonds. Transacting is easy. Liquidity represents the ability to buy and sell your individual holdings at a price that is acceptable to you. There are two key pieces to this definition. First, notice that I said "buy and sell." Second, and more importantly, you need to be able to transact at a price that is acceptable to you. An acceptable price to you is an important piece and is a significant differentiator in the marketplace. There is always someone to take the other side of a trade, but just because there is a buyer for your bond doesn't mean that the price is acceptable to you.

Not to pick on Lehman Brothers, but on the day that company declared bankruptcy, there were buyers of the debt. Unfortunately—or fortunately, depending on which side of the trade you were on—the price was somewhere in the range of 10 cents to 29 cents on the dollar. You may say that Lehman Brothers debt was a special occurrence. Well yes, it was; however, the demise of the company didn't just affect its debt. It sent shock waves throughout the markets, hitting the financial sector the hardest. Roughly two weeks after the financial crisis was near its peak, all financial institutions remained under pressure. That includes banks, brokers, insurance companies, and anyone else that might have had a financial arm. This list included the automakers, companies that make heavy machinery, and even some very diversified companies that have a finance arm. In some cases, the finance arm only existed to help a company execute its ongoing funding needs, to help it remain a going concern. The bottom line: Companies other than broker-dealers were negatively affected by the recent activity and moved lower in sympathy. In other words, these names were guilty by association. It shouldn't be a surprise that liquidity was a concern. The shock and lack of liquidity did not just affect the lower-rated or esoteric debt—that would have been too easy and sensible.

Higher-quality credits were impacted as well. Names from both the financial and nonfinancial sector were affected. One name in particular within the financial sector comes to mind. The company was a triple-A bank that issued and sold debt frequently to investors in the money market sector. The money market sector can be defined as the same time frame as the front end of the yield curve. There are different criteria that provide money market managers the ability to extend past the 13 months and buy longer-dated debt. Different structures, such as callable bonds and those with put dates, allow this to happen. I am not going to go into the details, but it is important to mention. At any rate, the triple-A bank's balance sheet was strong, very strong. Fundamentally, it was a sound institution deserving of its triple-A status. Where the breakdown occurred was within the markets. Investors or traders changed their perception of the bank. Thinking back, the perception of the bank might not have changed; what changed might have been how

risk was evaluated. I have to admit, my view at the macro level changed as
well. The red flags went up over the entire sector, just not fundamentally
for the company. Throughout the weeks the company remained strong and
a going concern. The company's profile didn't change. What did change
was how the equity market was falling, sharply impacting and taking along
with it the financial names, including the triple-A bank. Equity traders were
on a witch hunt looking for the next victim. Credit spreads were widening,
pushing prices to new and unheard-of levels for high-quality paper.

The triple-A bank that we owned matured in less than two weeks. To be
clear, that is less than 14 days. Due to all the volatility and uncertainty within
the financial sector, we shopped the bond to different dealers looking for a
bid. We were not necessarily looking to sell it. It was about price discovery.
Now let me frame this a bit further. We owned a bond that would mature
within days and carried a triple-A rating. The bond should have been trading
right around par, carrying a price of $100. The par amount of the bond was
roughly $50 million. It was not an odd lot that, in stressed times, will likely
receive a below-market bid. Unfortunately, the price that we received on our
round lot offer was nowhere near the level a triple-A, strong financial bank
should trade at—which is par. The price that was quoted from the dealer
community was around 80 cents on the dollar. 80 cents! We could have hit
the bid and sold the bond at this level but chose not to. It was tradable, but
did not offer very good liquidity. This is a prime example of how a bond
can be traded but still remain illiquid by my definition. Again, the important
piece is that the bond out for bid must receive an acceptable price. It is clear
that the 80-cent bid was not an acceptable price. We held the bond for the
remaining days and received par—100 cents on the dollar. It clearly makes
sense that, as an investor you are always searching for the best price. Don't
let anyone throw the blanket statement out there that the bond is liquid. Yes,
of course it is liquid, but at what price? In this case, the market environment
was hindering the liquidity of the bond. In some cases, the characteristics
of the bond may detract from its liquidity, and sometimes the entire sector
may be out of favor, which could negatively affect the ability for a bond to
be traded.

There are multiple reasons that a bond could become illiquid; some
inherent to the actual bond and, like in the example above, some due to the
environment impacting liquidity. Because there are so many factors that can
impact your bond's liquidity, remember to take advantage of what is given
to you. This is why it makes sense to use the sweet spot of the curve, if at
all possible. It is usually the most liquid holding with the highest probability
to receive best prices. One reason for this is that there are many different
buyers and different strategies that utilize the selected time frame.

CONSISTENT COUPONS

Capturing sizable coupons within fixed income investing is always very important, because a portion of your total return is driven from the income. Capturing sizable coupons in a laddered or low-turnover strategy is paramount. As we work through this section it will become apparent why it is so important to achieve the highest possible coupons. First, let's answer why it is so important to attain strong coupons. In a low-turnover or passive strategy, the investor is looking for income. More times than not, this income is used as a key contributor to performance. Preservation of capital and current income are attractive qualities to investors within these strategies. Coupons are generally not the focus in a total return strategy, whether it is in a mutual fund or separate account structure. Coupons may be part of the strategy; however, they play second fiddle to other strategy components.

Now that we have established that coupons are an integral component to a laddered strategy, we need to focus on the coupon itself. You might have noticed that I keep using the word strong when referring to the coupon. Why is that? Coupons, like anything else, have characteristics. A strong coupon may be looked at as greater than current market levels. The benefit: The income that is generated will be greater than the market average. The downfall: There may not be a great abundance or availability of these types of coupons. What is more important than the one bond that provides a higher coupon is finding the right mix of coupons to create that consistent stream of income. Finding that consistency within a portfolio that places a heavy emphasis on coupons sounds a lot easier to accomplish than it really is.

Consistency allows you to create and distribute a weighted average coupon at the portfolio level without having to overweight or underweight different parts of the yield curve. This is more important than you may think. If you deviate from the structure of the strategy, you chance losing the benefit of mitigating interest rate risk. It is not as simple as it may sound. Portions of interest rate risk may be gained or lost depending on the severity of the deficiency. As you know, the yield curve doesn't always shift in parallel fashion. It may steepen or flatten at various points. If the current allocation to the portfolio is under- or overweight in that section, your portfolio may be disadvantaged. With that said, it may work in your favor and you may be overweight the point of the curve that is rallying or underweight the point that is selling off. The problem is the uncertainty and the unknown that could create adverse end results for the portfolio.

Having the ability to invest and create a consistent coupon stream aids in reducing various risks and allows the portfolio, once implemented, to run in an efficient manner. It must be mentioned that there are times when a premium must be paid at the time of purchase. This usually happens in a bull market, when interest rates are moving lower and when companies are issuing debt or replacing or adding to existing debt. The higher premium that you pay will equalize the yield to maturity of the bond. The search for consistent coupons is imperative for consistent income.

For example, if the goal of the portfolio is to generate $500,000 in income a year, a $10,000,000 portfolio would need to have a weighted average coupon of five percent. In an ideal setting, the manager would be able to invest in bonds that all carry a five percent coupon. This is not always possible, for many reasons. Usually when constructing a well-diversified portfolio, investments are made over the course of several weeks. This is also determined by the strategy that the manager is implementing. For instance, a Treasury-only or government portfolio will take far less time to invest than a state-specific municipal portfolio. Over time, as interest rates move, volatility is created and within volatility comes an interest rate roller coaster ride. This ride usually will create an environment that is not conducive to finding consistent coupons. There is, however, a greater likelihood of accomplishing this with a ladder implemented in the sweet spot of the curve.

WHY IS SUPPLY IMPORTANT?

First, supply is a term that is used to describe bonds that are available for purchase. You may have heard this expressed in other ways as well, such as new issue calendar and visible supply. Supply is the amount of issuance that is brought to market. It is the number of bonds that companies offer to investors in the marketplace, measured on a daily basis or aggregated to yearly figures. It is straightforward—the larger the supply is, the more bonds that are available for purchase. What needs to be assessed and determined is the net supply amount. This is exactly what it sounds like. The net amount is the difference between new supply brought to market and the amount of debt that is retiring. For instance, if there is $200 billion of new supply brought to the market, that might sound like a lot (or it may not). In all seriousness, if $100 billion of the supply is replacing $100 billion of bonds that are maturing, you only have $100 billion of net new issuance. Now the number doesn't look as significant. Trends also need to be looked for, as history paints a picture of supply trends. If you look back over 2011, issuance totaled 858.1 billion. Net issuance was 460.6 billion (data according to Barclays Capital). If you track the data, trends will start to appear. Think about it this way: If you know that supply increased every March, you should be able to structure and build your portfolio with maturities to coincide with the months that provide ample supply. The greater the number of bonds for purchase, the better diversified the portfolio is. If you were in the market for a new car, would you go to the dealer that has three cars on the lot to choose from? No, you would go to the auto dealer with 300. The same holds true when buying bonds: The greater the supply, the more options you have for your portfolio. Think back to the discussion about the front end of the curve and how the majority of issuance was from the financial sector. If 60 percent of your portfolio is invested in the financial sector, you may feel that your portfolio is not well diversified. You would not want to run into this scenario unless you are building a highly concentrated or specialized portfolio. The bottom line is that supply is important because it allows you to better diversify your portfolio and invest in an efficient manner.

Supply comes in waves, and this is one area where history is able to help predict future activity. Each sector has its own unique trends and supply activity. August, for example, is well known in the industry as the summer month that is very slow. Activity is almost nonexistent. The running joke is that the market and Wall Street shut down. Traders, analysts, and portfolio managers are using the remaining warm summer days to hit the beach. And just like that, the new issue calendar dries up. However, the first week of September usually brings an onslaught of new deals. Patience is rewarded if you wait. As an investor, it is in your best interest not to fund or fully implement a strategy toward the end of summer if you do not need to. It pays to wait.

There is another time of the year when investors can count on seeing additional supply. This time around, it is from the government and in the form of Treasury securities. Fast forward six months from the end of August. We're now in the February-to-March time frame. Around this time every year, the market is hit with an abundance of new supply from the U.S. T-bill market, as the government issues additional debt leading up to Tax Day. This is important because with additional supply there are likely more sellers than buyers, or not enough buyers to take down all the debt. This imbalance creates an environment where prices fall, pushing yields higher. Dealer balance sheets are full, and in order to reduce them, they must cheapen the bills to try to entice additional buyers. This occurred in February 2012. U.S. Treasury bills were carrying a negative yield to 10 basis points, depending on what maturity you were looking at. Prior to the backup, one-year bills were paying 8 to 10 basis points, and the one-month bill around 5 to 6 basis points. What paltry yields. This was the period when Greece was on the verge of defaulting and the Fed was anchoring the front end at zero interest rates. To start, whether interest rates were at 10 basis points or five percent, the pickup for extending your maturity 11 months was not really significant.

Remember that yields, particularly in the front end of the Treasury curve, were at historic lows. They were supported at these levels by the loose monetary policy and ongoing threat of default by Greece or any of the European financial institutions. At these low levels, it almost seems not even worth mentioning for a couple of basis points. In this type of environment, a couple of basis points can make or break your year. Prepare for a backup in yields by temporarily building a larger percentage of cash ready to take advantage of the yield dislocations. This period in time creates an excellent buying opportunity on the backups or dips.

The construction of the ladder takes one shape and one shape only. This is the even distribution of bonds across a set time frame. Although a ladder can be constructed over any time frame, short or long, the front end of the curve or long end, the sweet spot is the optimal spot for implementation. A ladder strategy can utilize different asset classes that range from Treasuries to municipal securities, and potentially, anything in between.

PERFORMANCE AND HOW TO MEASURE IT

In this day and age, everyone and everything is measured on performance. Individuals at their place of employment are measured on their productivity—a form of performance. Computers are measured on the speed of the processor. What about cars? Let's stick with the speed theme. One performance measurement for a car is how fast it goes. What is its top speed? If you line up a high-performance sports car against a sport utility vehicle, chances are the sports car is going to outperform the sport utility on the straightaway. Let's be serious, the sports car will blow it away. It is a faster car. But what happens if we take the race off-road where there is not a smooth surface, there is mud and brush. There is a greater chance that the sport utility will be victorious. One reason the sport utility outperforms the sports car this time around is that there is a different set of circumstances. Each car is a winner under a particular set of circumstances or rules. Just as there are different ways to measure performance when judging cars, it is a similar story when measuring investment portfolios.

The question that I am always asked is, what is the most appropriate way to capture and measure portfolio performance? Just like in the example of the sports car racing the sport utility, it depends on the surroundings. If you use your imagination, what needs to happen is to swap out the mud and brush for the investment policy statement that outlines the portfolio characteristics or portfolio surroundings. Within the fixed income world, there are different categories that strategies fall under. Looking down from above, there are actively managed strategies and passively managed strategies. There are ways to measure performance on both styles. As you may have guessed, a different road needs to be taken for each style, because each style has different characteristics. At first, you need to take a step back as it may be difficult to gather the different attributes that need to be analyzed. Different strategies have unique and inherent goals that require an open mind to performance measurement. I say an open mind because depending on the strategy goals, you may need to think outside the box on how to judge and measure the portfolio. This is not an overnight process and may take some time to figure out. No matter how much time and effort is required, it is imperative to figure this out so that an accurate assessment can take place.

LOW-TURNOVER DILEMMA

Measuring performance is an age-old conundrum as it relates to passive or low-turnover fixed income strategies. As just mentioned, the question that is always asked is what is the best way to judge the account? Should the investor grade the manager? The simple answer is yes, but how? Should the manager be measured on how he or she does versus a benchmark? If so, what benchmark? Should the portfolio be judged on how much income it generates, its yield, or a combination of any of the above? All of these characteristics can be measured. The difficult decision is which characteristics to use, and then, how to measure them. When deciding how you plan to measure the portfolios, keep in mind the basics. This is where the customization comes into play. Don't lose sight of the strategy's goal. If the primary goal is the preservation of capital, and the income the strategy generates is secondary, these should be incorporated in the performance measurement. This is an important notion: to look at performance in a different light. The traditional way investors measure the performance of a manager is to calculate alpha.

Too many investors get hung up on the alpha concept. Alpha is the portfolio's excess return over a stipulated benchmark. This concept is not a proper way to measure performance for all strategies. For an active strategy, yes, absolutely, calculating how a manager generated alpha and the amount is the proper measurement. However, a laddered bond strategy is run in a passive manner. This strategy has a very low turnover ratio and is not run in a total return fashion. This should be no surprise, due to the usual goals of this type of mandate. In the end, the return of the portfolio should be measured with other goals that are more in line with the strategy goal and not alpha in its typical sense.

Aside from a total return bond fund, in a low-turnover or passive strategy, there should not be a return or alpha target and there should be no benchmark used to manage against. Take out the notion of managing and the need of a benchmark and you head off many problems. I know because I have dealt with numerous questions on this topic. It is sometimes difficult for the end client to grasp this concept. This concept easily becomes confusing to some investors because performance and alpha target are ingrained into everyone's head as soon as they are old enough to understand what an investment is. It is understandable, because investors are brainwashed with stock market ideals and commonality, as equity portfolios are measured versus a benchmark, striving for alpha.

A laddered strategy is an investment that is a long-term solution that provides the preservation of capital and current income. Because the portfolio carries these two characteristics, performance needs to be measured in a way that captures these traits. One way I like to assess the success of a portfolio is to look at and compare the yield at purchase of the portfolio to the yield of a market benchmark. I use the yield at purchase over current yield or yield to maturity to measure the success of the strategy. This measure is important. For a strategy that has little to no turnover, efficiencies are one way to garner strong performance.

SUCCESS OF A STRATEGY

The trade and executed price will drive the success of the strategy. Driven by capitalizing on dislocations at the security level, you must create a strategy with a higher yield at purchase than the current market yield to represent a successful solution. The yield at purchase is chosen because a well-implemented portfolio has little to no turnover. The yield to maturity takes into account the current market price and provides a snapshot of the portfolio, but not an accurate read of the overall portfolio yield. Using the current market price represents a yield that an investor would expect to capture if the portfolio was funded at that point in time. From that viewpoint, it is clear why that information is good information to have, but not relevant to the portfolio performance. Since the goal of this strategy is to have minimal turnover, new securities will not be added to the portfolio on a regular basis. There will be additions when bonds mature; however, not in the interim through the new issue calendar or dislocations arising from market volatility—two components that impact an index.

If you are set on measuring your portfolio by the amount of alpha it generates, you will need to set a benchmark to measure it against. There are many different indexes to choose from. The important aspect of choosing an index is to pick one that represents your goals and the characteristics of your portfolio accurately. What I mean by this is that you would not want to use an all-Treasury index if your portfolio holds corporate government and mortgage debt. (Well, you may, however it would not be a true comparison.) Also make sure the characteristics are the same, or at least similar. You don't want to compare your portfolio that is invested in the sweet spot of the yield curve to an index that has 30 percent allocation to the 30-year part of the curve. This type of inconsistency will likely create havoc on calculating performance attribution. If needed, go back to Chapter 10, "The Yield Curve," as it will provide the different shapes of the curve and potential impacts. There are many different index providers, so the task in finding one that is a good fit should not be too difficult. If using a benchmark is the path you choose, I can't stress enough: Make sure that you are comparing apples to apples with your index and portfolio.

CHAPTER 12

Alternatives to a Traditional Ladder Strategy

Buy right and hold tight.

—John C. Bogle

This chapter is geared to provide alternatives or options for funding purposes in the creation of a low-turnover or laddered bond strategy. A traditional taxable laddered strategy employs the U.S. Treasury sector. This is a strong and suitable strategy when the market looks attractive, but what should be used when the Treasury market looks frothy and does not look very promising? A perfect example is the 2011 time frame. Interest rates were at ultralow levels and in some cases, prices were at all-time highs. This is a terrific example of when the Treasury sector may not look as attractive as other sectors or asset classes for a variety of reasons. Treasury yields may not look very enticing for a number of reasons, such as an outright price level, or even from a yield to maturity standpoint. A low-yield environment can be detrimental to a fixed income investor. This type of environment is capable of deterring many investors from putting their money to work as frustration sets in. Many investors see the low-yield environment as problematic, because fixed income investors usually use the proceeds from the coupon or yield calculation as income or as a part of the total return calculation. From 2008 through mid-2012, yields within the Treasury market continued trending lower. It wouldn't surprise me if this pitfall of low yields felt by investors doesn't abate anytime soon. It may continue well into 2014. This environment was caused by a number of factors. It might be coincidental that all these factors lined up. There will always be someone saying that it was one in a million, a perfect storm, or "next time it will be different." This type of situation happens more frequently than you may think, though.

During the period from 2008 through mid-2012, there were a handful of investment banks that closed their doors, and oil shot up over $100 a barrel, not once, but multiple times. The U.S. economy entered a recession, exited a recession, and teetered on the brink of falling back into a recession. A second recession likely would have occurred if not for the U.S. government bailing out the country by injecting billions and billions of dollars into the markets and banking system. In addition, the European Union was being tested, as members of the eurozone were having similar problems. Economies within countries across Europe were faltering as government debt was skyrocketing, leading to significant risks within the eurozone. Countries were, at times, just days away from a sovereign default, which continued to call into question the sustainability of the European Union. If that was not enough, as discussed earlier, the United States of America lost its AAA rating from one of the Big Three rating agencies.

I am not trying to paint a negative picture—though you might not believe that based on the preceding statements. It is just so hard to comprehend, if you are not engulfed in the thick of things on a daily basis, how many headwinds there really are. There are so many minor threats that complicate the picture but never make the Main Street headlines. For instance, how many headlines were there announcing that the government auction was potentially days away from not happening and European countries were on the edge of default? As a result of this, the equity markets spun out of control, falling fast and furious, but of course the papers didn't run that headline. If a newspaper did print the headline, it would likely have provided an abbreviated statement reading "Government Debt Auction Almost Failed," and the article would not have elaborated much. The next possible ramifications of the failed auction would not have been presented. Out of the headwinds discussed, what would have been the odds that all these occurrences would have happened together? Not in your wildest dreams. Taking this a step further, how many of those same headwinds would you have thought could happen simultaneously or within a span of a few months? Not to state the obvious, but the answer is not many, if any at all. This short summary of the events that occurred over the past three years is a clear example of one primary reason for why interest rates remained at abnormally low levels for the time period. It is important to understand: The chain of events is important. It is not the actual events that raise the eyebrow, it is the possibility of simultaneous events occurring that have an adverse effect on the markets. With Treasury yields specifically at abnormally low levels, this is an example of when an investor may look toward other investments as alternatives to Treasuries. There are higher quality alternatives to investing within the Treasury market. This section will talk about these alternatives, which carry a similar high quality rating. Comfort should remain solid, because some alternatives even carry an explicit guarantee from the U.S. government, while others carry an implicit guarantee.

TIPS: THE OTHER TREASURY

Treasury inflation-protected securities (TIPS) provide investors another opportunity to invest in a U.S. government security that holds the explicit guarantee of the U.S. government. At this point, some investors might feel that the backing does not mean as much as it did a year ago, when it was still rated triple-A. Even at double-A rating from Standard & Poor's (S&P), the U.S. government is still the U.S. government, which provides an explicit guarantee—just as it does on its nominal Treasury debt.

There are additional benefits inherent to these securities. Not only do TIPS carry the explicit guarantee of the U.S. government, they also provide protection against the erosion of your purchasing power through the increase of inflation or expectation of future inflationary pressures. This inflation protection could be looked at as an added bonus due to the fact that the inflation adjustment provides protection from the loss of your dollar's purchasing power.

Each investor has his or her own reason for utilizing the TIPS market. In my opinion, the number one reason is to protect investments from the erosion of purchasing power due to inflation. This is accomplished through adjustments due to inflation measured by the consumer price index (CPI). The coupons are not adjusted, but the principal amount of your investment is adjusted on a monthly basis when the CPI is reported. It is important to focus on the non-seasonally adjusted CPI report and not get confused, by the multiple variations of this indicator. This feature is very beneficial when portfolios are confronted with an economic environment that is poised for growth, which has the ability to generate inflationary pressures. Whether the economy is running on all cylinders or is in another stage of the economic cycle, the prospects of inflation are around. One of the few times inflation might not be on investors' minds is when the economy is projecting a deflationary outcome. Except for deflationary times—that is, when inflation is below zero as prices are decreasing—inflation is usually around and always a concern. It is just a matter of to what extent, or the extent of erosion, that creates uncertainty and fear within the markets. The erosion of pricing power is a critical impairment to a portfolio. If inflation is on the rise and uncertainty is present, creating speculation, a move higher in price is likely to happen.

Accommodative monetary policy is a driver which is created by the Federal Open Market Committee (FOMC). The FOMC and an accommodative policy are discussed in detail in Chapter 8. It is, however, worth noting again that the FOMC has the mandate to attempt to control inflation. The more restrictive the committee's policy becomes, the less likely it is for inflation to materialize. These are important concepts to understand when owning TIPS.

A secondary reason may be the level of comfort that you gain knowing that you own a highly rated security backed by the U.S. government. There is another reason that I find very enticing that is easily overlooked. Price movement of TIPS does not track to its nominal counterpart on a one-for one basis. What you have is a situation of two Treasury securities with some similar characteristics that do not always act in similar fashion. The two securities are not correlated on a one-to-one basis. This means that they will act differently in different environments. This feature may be very beneficial if utilized at the right time.

Break-Even Opportunity

A 10-year TIPS provides a "real" yield of 1.0 percent. At first glance, that doesn't look as compelling as the 3.4 percent nominal yield that a conventional Treasury is providing. If future inflation were to run at 2.5 percent, then the real yield of the 10-year note should drop to only 0.9 percent (3.4 percent − 2.5 percent = 0.9 percent). At 0.9 percent on the nominal Treasury, the TIPS that initially looked less attractive at 1.0 percent is now more compelling. The other way to look at this is from a break-even perspective. The break-even rate is the difference between the nominal yield and the yield on the TIPS. In this case, 3.4 percent −1.0 percent = 2.4 percent. The end result is the same at 2.4 percent. If you believe that inflation will run hotter over the duration of the security—in this case, higher than 2.4 percent—the TIPS looks attractive.

Asset managers and traders may also at times utilize the TIPS market as a hedge against rising interest rates. There are other methods to hedge against rising interest rates that may better protect your investment from the adverse effects of rising rates. If your portfolio is confined to government securities in the cash market, in my opinion, TIPS are one of your best bets. This trade ranks very high in my book, because you receive all the benefits of a U.S. Treasury security, plus principal adjustments for inflation. The hedge aspect is introduced through the beta of the security.

Measured over a four-year time frame, from December 31, 2007, to December 31, 2011, the five-year TIPS holds a .70 beta and .675 correlation to its nominal counterpart. This is telling us that for every 100 basis points (bps) or one percent move higher in nominal or conventional Treasury rates, the five-year TIPS will move .70 percent, calculated on the price change of

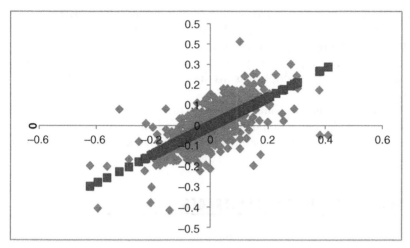

FIGURE 12.1   Sample of the Five-Year TIPS
Source: Bloomberg data.

each security. Figure 12.1 shows the sample taken over the time period has a strong correlation as there are minimal outliers. Ideally, all of the observations would fall on the mean (the straight line). Simply put, this shows us that the data are reliable and a strong fit.

For a moment, take the inflation component out of the equation and look at how this may perform in a rising-rate environment. The Treasury allocation that is in your investment portfolio might benefit from exposure to the TIPS market. Currently, we live in a world of low interest rates and low-inflation. There will be a time when interest rates will move higher. It may be in a methodical and measured process, or an erratic backup. Adding exposure to the TIPS sector protects you against any type of backup in rates. If you take a look further back in history, the beta of .70 percent turns into .81 percent. In a rising interest rate environment, I will take this relationship any day, while still holding on to the benefits of the Treasury sector. As with anything, there is the potential downside to the TIPS sector, though. It is not always just roses. TIPS will lag conventional Treasuries in a rally. On the flip side, for every 100 bps or one percent rally in rates, the TIPS will lag the market and move only .7 percent. As an investor and holder of a Treasury security, you will still receive the benefit of any flight-to-quality rally. The move will be muted due to the beta, unless of course, there are concerns about inflation. What investors have going for them in today's market is that they are less likely to see conventional Treasuries rally from current levels. Due to support from global central banks and the specter of inflation—regardless whether it is today's, tomorrow's, or a problem two years from now—a sell-off carries a higher probability, at least in my eyes.

Whatever the reason, inflation protection or an allocation within your fixed income portfolio, TIPS may be an essential part to achieve your goal. As discussed, there are multiple reasons that an allocation to the TIPS market is imperative.

At any time, the economic landscape may change and inflation can rear its ugly head. Higher commodity prices and an overly accommodative monetary policy have the capability to create havoc and push ultralow interest rates higher.

CONSIDER MBS POOLS OF MORTGAGES

Mortgage-backed securities (MBS) provide a portfolio a way to potentially add incremental yield. There are varying types, including agency and nonagency. What exactly does that mean? Although fairly simple, it is not necessarily intuitive. An implicit or explicit guarantee from the U.S. government is the dividing line between the two classifications. Agency mortgages are those securities that carry a direct or indirect guarantee by the U.S. government, whereas nonagency debt is issued by private entities and does not have government support. Securities that have the backing of the government, or an implied backstop, trade differently from those that do not. Similar to other spread products, this is most noticeable when there is stress within the marketplace. In addition, both types of MBS perform differently from your typical fixed income security. To start, MBS securities pay income on a monthly basis, whereas most, but not all, fixed income securities carry a semiannual coupon. A portfolio constructed for income could benefit from adding these securities and is another way to diversify your portfolio. These securities normally carry a higher yield than a Treasury security, and sometimes, even higher than a corporate note. The higher yield is garnered from the pool of mortgages that are packaged together to form the security.

It has become more difficult, whether from a psychological factor or otherwise, to invest within the MBS market. This can be chalked up to the problems within the housing market. If you take a long-term approach on mortgage-backed investing, purchasing Ginnie Mae security is usually a safe play. One reason for this is the guarantee that comes along with Ginnie Mae securities because they are fully backed by the U.S. government.

Nonagency MBS deals are issued by a private institution and potentially, have an attractive yield, usually over agency MBS. This is because the underlying mortgages are not conforming. That is, they do not qualify for issuance through Fannie Mae, Freddie Mac, or other government-sponsored entities. These types of MBS are considered to carry a higher degree of risk due to the underlying loans, and the fact that they do not have a tie, direct or indirect, to the U.S. government. Nonagency MBS require a significant amount of credit work. If done properly, the analysis can become a very tedious process, and an argument can be made for utilizing a manager that specializes in these types of securities.

Similar to other fixed income securities, there is a relationship between MBS and interest rates, but with an added twist. Regarding agency MBS where the credit risk is mitigated due to the issuer, when interest rates decline, there is the possibility that mortgage owners will be quick to refinance their current loans. When borrowers refinance their loans, the underlying mortgages are paid off sooner than anticipated, reducing the principal amount of the pool. This would create what is called prepayment risk—prepaying your mortgage before the full term, which affects MBS and could affect investors within the MBS market in a negative way. For instance, if rates are high, your MBS investment is clipping a nice coupon of 6 percent. Interest rates are now rallying and moving lower. Uncertainty starts to set in about the homeowners of the underlying mortgages starting to refinance and lock in the lower rate. This is obviously a positive if you are the homeowner, but not necessarily a good thing if you are a bond holder. If the homeowners of the loans that are pooled together all start to refinance, the prepayment speed of the bond will increase. A greater prepayment speed will reduce the security's original face at a faster rate. Your investment will be returned sooner and the coupon that was locked in will now generate a smaller amount of income than before. The high coupon that you thought was going to sustain the life of the bond is no longer. There is another downside to this equation as well. If rates are low and start to move higher in the opposite direction, homeowners are not as likely to pay off their loans as quickly. There is no great incentive to refinance, because rates are higher. Another factor that must be considered when analyzing these types of securities is the state of the homeowner. It is important to follow whether the homeowner is staying current on the outstanding note. If the loans within the pools are becoming delinquent, a red flag should go up and evaluation of the current environment should commence.

MBS are an attractive alternative to a traditional laddered or passively managed account. For these types of accounts, these securities are most attractive in a predictable (as predictable a market can be) range-bound environment.

CONSIDER CORPORATE BONDS

The corporate sector is another way to shift away from government securities and add diversification to your portfolio. Adding credit exposure or implementing a corporate bond strategy will help diversify your fixed income allocation, and also attain a pickup in incremental yield. There was always a concern about liquidity when investing in the corporate bond market. This was rampant in the retail or high net worth space. The lack of size was known to hinder smaller portfolios. Asset managers who only managed accounts for individuals had a more difficult time sourcing bonds because they were limited to the number of dealers that were made available to them. There was always someone who was willing to sell you a bond regardless of the size. It became much more problematic when you were looking for someone to buy back that bond that had been sold to you. As electronic trading became more mainstream and prevalent within the marketplace, there was an liquidity increased. With the changing of the guard on Wall Street and the entrance of many smaller dealers, trading changed dramatically. Trading by invitation-only started to occur. This meant dealers were not adding positions to their balance sheets. It also meant that a trade would not occur unless there was another interested party to take the other side of the trade. This type of activity predominantly takes place right after dislocations within the marketplace. The environment has loosened up, but is still present on a lesser scale. The beneficial outcome to the buy side was that everyone was clamoring for trading activity. Asset managers and the accounts benefited from the increased attention and ability to receive institutional pricing on smaller lots.

In general, corporate bond portfolios, regardless of the direction of interest rates, may provide additional pickup in yield; therefore, they benefit your laddered portfolio, as income is generated from the coupons. Interest rates may rise, fall, or even remain unchanged, and credit provides diversification and the potential for additional yield over the Treasury. It is fair to say that if interest rates move higher, fixed income securities in general will be negatively affected. Corporate securities may feel the pain, as yields broadly will move higher. If you are comparing corporate securities to the Treasury sector, it is a different story. The increased diversification that a corporate bond provides a portfolio should help the portfolio weather the storm better. This is based on two assumptions that add appeal to the sector. First, the additional pickup in yield, or what is known as the spread, over Treasuries is realized and captured over a Treasury with a like duration or maturity characteristics. Second is that as the economy remains on solid footing or shows signs of improving, for example post a slowdown, the expectation is that corporate balance sheets also improve. We know this relationship exists because corporate securities are impacted directly by the health of the economy, and more importantly the health of the company issuing the debt. The price action of the corporate security and spread is also driven by the fundamental health of the company's balance sheet. The benefit of owning corporate securities was witnessed over the past year through the compression of yield spreads (the difference between corporate yields and Treasury yield) in 2011 . The spread tightening was—and usually is—a choppy ride. But remember, that doesn't matter to an investor who is using these securities within a laddered bond portfolio. Volatility is not a primary concern, or possibly, even a concern at all to an investor in this strategy, because they are looking for added diversification and to capture that additional yield that will help provide the income the investor is looking for.

In 2009, the demise of Lehman Brothers rocked the credit world. In 2010, volatility was driven by the antigovernment protests in the Middle East and Africa and higher oil prices all impacting the economic recovery. 2011 was a slightly different story, with the European financial crisis and sovereign debt crisis dominating the headlines. It doesn't matter whether the economy is in a recovery mode or another stage within the business cycle; these types of hiccups could arise at any time, creating unnecessary volatility. Markets are sensitive to disruptions, dislocations, and most of all, uncertainty. The key to investing within the corporate sector in a passive or laddered account is to keep an eye on corporate balance sheets and not get caught up in the day-to-day volatility and exogenous events that you can't control. This type of activity will drive yields within the corporate sector, impacting the portfolio. In the end, you are striving to achieve diversification and an increased yield by adding corporate credit exposure to your portfolio.

FLOATING-RATE NOTES

Corporate floating-rate notes are another way to diversify holdings, not only as an investment strategy, but also within the corporate sector. A floating-rate note strategy is designed to mitigate interest rate risk, which helps protect the portfolio from a rising interest rate environment. This is accomplished through the inherent characteristics of each security. Before we dive into the characteristics of the individual securities, it is worth noting that the same fundamental approach can be taken when assessing the floating-rate note market as you would use in the fixed corporate sector. Credit analysis is required and corporate balance sheets need to analyzed, looking for strengths and weaknesses. Careful attention needs to be paid to the company's cash and liquidity positions.

There are many different structures of floating-rate notes. Varieties are driven by the coupon and the reset structure or schedule. A standard floating-rate note structure has its coupon reset tied to either the one-month or three-month London Interbank Offered Rate (LIBOR). What does this mean? Coupons will keep pace with rising rates. This is accomplished by having each coupon associated with the floating-rate note security fixed off of the LIBOR rate on the reset day. For an example, a General Electric Capital Corp. note was issued with a coupon of three-month LIBOR plus 12.5 bps. The first coupon was .4725 percent; therefore, the three-month LIBOR was .3475. That is, LIBOR + .125 bps, or .3475 + .125. The initial margin remains constant, but the daily spread to LIBOR can change due to market activity.

What Is LIBOR?

LIBOR is the perceived rate at which banks are able to borrow funds at from one another. There are a select number of banks that sit on the LIBOR panel that provide input to determine the appropriate level. After eliminating the four highest and four lowest rates, the remaining rates are averaged to come up with the LIBOR level. The LIBOR rate is usually set just before 11:00 A.M. London time. For instance, a two-year floating-rate note may be priced at three-month LIBOR plus 10 basis points.

A Deeper Look at LIBOR

Let's examine LIBOR at a deeper level, including recent trends. As of early 2012, according to the British Bankers Association (BBA), there were 18 banks that contribute to setting the U.S. dollar LIBOR rate. These banks are known as the member panel banks. The U.S. dollar LIBOR rate is driven by the daily rate that these banks feel they are able to borrow funds at. It is common to have different contributing banks that set the LIBOR level in different currencies. There are 16 banks that set the British pound LIBOR level, and only 11 banks that are involved in the setting of the Canadian dollar LIBOR level. Similar to how the general markets perform, volatility is low when stress is absent from the system. Unfortunately, this is not always the case. We have seen significant volatility over the past few years, as U.S. and European banks and financial institutions ran into difficulties. As troubles grew, banks found that they needed to manage ongoing solvency concerns, which at times, was a very arduous task. This all took place while the global economy attempted to find its footing, bouncing back and forth between expansion and contraction, or threat of contraction. As a result, LIBOR skyrocketed, as banks were leery of lending to one another.

LIBOR has a tendency to respond to volatility and uncertainty within the marketplace. In addition, LIBOR tends to track FOMC activity. Figure 12.2 shows this relationship over the past decade.

We are coming to a crossroads. The FOMC has held rates low for years, which has artificially pulled LIBOR lower. There have been a few occurrences when LIBOR has trended in the opposite direction of the Fed, moving

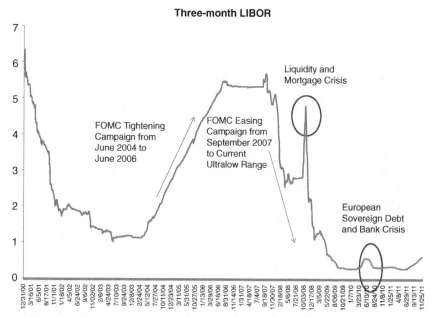

FIGURE 12.2   Three-Month LIBOR and FOMC Activity
Source: Bloomberg data.

higher. Today's environment is sending many diverging signals. We know that the FOMC has orchestrated a zero interest rate policy, and is unlikely to move from this stance in the near term. European financial institutions continue to face multiple headwinds, including funding issues driven by concerns of sovereign debt default. These factors, when put together, create uncertainties about global growth, while U.S. economic growth is pointing in the positive direction. There are multiple factors that could drive LIBOR higher from current levels. There is the view that interest rates will start to rise from the current low levels. When this move commences, there is a strong likelihood that LIBOR will follow. If LIBOR leads the march higher, it will likely be due to the uncertainties and fear within the marketplace. This could be largely driven by concern about the health of a financial institution. Figure 12.2 shows that LIBOR started to tick higher at the end of 2011. This move can be attributed to more-favorable U.S. economic data and the markets' view that the Fed would embark on a tightening campaign, removing some of the cheap money that had been injected into the system. At the same time, the front end of the yield curve remained tied to ultralow levels due to the current Fed policy. The fact that LIBOR can lead the markets higher or Fed activity will initiate the move is an important piece to consider when investing in corporate floating-rate notes.

This is an important consideration to hold on to, as discussed in earlier chapters: The FOMC sets the overall direction of interest rates and has the ability to manipulate the markets, directly or on an indirect basis. This is an important concept to understand when investing within the floating-rate note market. It is a key piece to track if there is the expectation that interest rates will move higher in the near term. Historically, in a stable low volatile interest rate environment, LIBOR trades with a positive spread to Fed funds. The relationship between three-month LIBOR and the fed funds target rate, looking back to 1992, is consistent with increased volatility in recent years. Over that time period, the spread averaged 27 bps above the fed funds target rate. Throughout the decades, the markets were hit with many adversities, with which you can gauge the magnitude of the dislocation by the difference between the average spread and current spread. Interestingly enough, in the time period right before the mortgage storm—that is, from 2004 to 2006—the spread averaged 29 bps as well. At the height of the turmoil, when panic hit in the street in 2008, the average spread increased to 83 bps for the year. This move, however, was significantly affected by the FOMC's activity. The Fed took the target rate from 4.25 percent at the beginning of the year down to the historic low of 25 bps. During that time, Treasuries followed, rallying for the year. If your portfolio was yield oriented, LIBOR-based products were the place to be, and not the Treasury market. The opposite held true if you were looking for total return. The Treasury sector had a fantastic run that year, before reversing course in 2009.

THE BOTTOMING PROCESS

Historical analysis from the past two recessions also shows that three-month LIBOR usually bottoms out approximately 18 to 20 months after the recession ends. The last recession, which started in December 2007 and ended in June 2009, was the longest since World War II. Early in the first quarter of 2011 marked the beginning of when LIBOR, according to the past two occurrences, should have started to make its climb higher, and we did see the modest uptick in three-month LIBOR toward the end of the second quarter. This move was almost in line and on track to fall within that 18- to 20-month window. This is a great example of how to take historical trends and relate them to the current situation. As you can see, it is more an art than a science. Nothing is a guarantee. This time, the move started around the two-year mark. The move itself was moderate due to the Fed's easy monetary policy. In the environment of ultralow rates, a pickup of 10- to

20 bps over Treasuries and some fixed rate corporate debt makes a significant difference to a portfolio. The incremental yield is notable. The move likely would have continued, and I would have expected it to accelerate, if not for activity from the FOMC called Operation Twist, which pushed the rate back down, though still trending higher.

I viewed floating-rate notes to be attractive in the first quarter of 2011. Yes, I was a couple of months early, but as we all know, it is very difficult to time or pick the bottom in any markets, whether it is the equity markets or fixed income markets. An allocation to the floating-rate note sector benefits from a move up in LIBOR, but LIBOR can move higher for different reasons, and the floating-rate notes do not show a bias to the reason. Not only does a healthy environment have the potential to push LIBOR rates higher, but as mentioned earlier, strains within the markets have the ability to create a slow march higher.

In 2010 and 2011, the European banking sector remained under pressure, as concerns about sovereign default circled. These concerns created multiple headaches that investors had to get a handle on. If the stress within the system continues to build, bank funding and government financing may become more and more difficult to obtain. As difficulty grows, the expectation would be for LIBOR to move higher, representing the added risk within the markets. Again, corporate floaters or floating-rate notes in general are not concerned about why LIBOR is moving higher, just that it is. What investors need to be cognizant of is if LIBOR is moving higher as a result of a credit event. Thorough credit analysis needs to take place to ensure the credit exposure remains strong at the security level.

LIBOR is one of the most widely used benchmarks for corporate floating-rate notes. It is also used as a gauge measuring credit risk within the financial system. I keep referencing when Lehman Brothers fell on hard times. When Lehman was forced to close its doors, LIBOR jumped over 200 bps, reflecting the perceived risk within the marketplace. On the other hand, when the banking system is healthy and functioning properly, LIBOR will remain constant, averaging 29 bps over Fed funds.

There are other benchmarks that are utilized; however, LIBOR is the most common. Others include a spread off of fed funds effective, or prime, rate, for instance. As interest rates rise or fall, the coupon of these securities will adjust, just as it would with LIBOR. For this reason, floating-rate note securities are attractive when interest rates are expected to rise. Coupon resets help investors hedge interest rate risk, protecting the investment.

CHAPTER **13**

Credit Analysis

Risk comes from not knowing what you are doing.
—Warren Buffett

Over the years, rating agencies have played an integral part in the investment community. They have made good calls, and of course, questionable calls as well. Truth be told, they are only human, but they are expected to provide accurate information, particularly when there is a fee attached to the service. At one point in time many years ago, there was the view held by some, that before any bond other than a U.S. Treasury was purchased, you only needed to look at the credit ratings to assess the overall health of the company that was issuing the debt. This was the perceived notion; however, just like anything else, times have changed.

In many ways, a bond rating paints a picture for the investor of the bonds that are available for purchase. Using the descriptive information provided by the rating agencies on a bond, you as a manager should, with a little homework, be able to understand the overall financial picture or health of the security. In addition, from the information provided, the management team should be able to deduce the necessary pieces to construct a view on the bond and at what level it should be trading.

THE AGENCY

Investors look to three primary rating agencies in the marketplace. There are others, but I will focus only on what I consider the top three. They are Moody's, Standard and Poor's (S&P), and Fitch. All three of these agencies have a ratings scale that covers the full spectrum of debt, from defaulted to the highest rating, triple-A. The three agencies do not have to be in agreement with each other on the quality of a bond. Many times they are not, but there is normally not a significant disparity between ratings. For example, one agency may rate at bond as a single-A, while another rates it as double-A Each company is analyzing the current financial health of the company, and for this reason, it is highly unlikely that one agency deems the company to be strong and another rating agency views the company as weak. When the agencies apply their forecasts to future growth, the assumptions that they use may differ, therefore impacting the ratings. Throughout history, there have been occasions—and there will be more in the future—when a bond is given conflicting ratings from different agencies. Times of stress and uncertainty usually provide imbalances in the marketplace, which might drive mixed ratings for a company. With that said, it would be very uncharacteristic and unlikely to have ratings that are at opposite ends of the spectrum—that range from a triple-A rating to a below-investment-grade.

History unfortunately has shown how rating activity impacts the market and investor viewpoints. It is customary for the agencies to change their view at times. I am not faulting them for that by any stretch of the imagination. Markets change, as do fundamentals within corporate balance sheets and, for example, municipalities. Rating agencies seemed to have a knack for changing their view or making sweeping broad changes at the worst possible time. The intentions are good; it just never seems to work out well. The worst possible time is usually when the markets are stressed, whatever the reason may be. And why not? The markets are in a volatile state; it makes complete sense to add a bit more uncertainty to the mix. In the past, agencies have at times taken sweeping action across a sector in full or in part, taking hundreds of securities down all at once.

The agencies do not discriminate by asset class or sector. Downgrades can affect the corporate sector or the municipal sector. Two recent examples come to the top of the list. S&P took down the ratings of hundreds of structured securities and mortgage bonds in a short time frame between late 2007 and 2008. This was the start of the credit crunch. Another notable event was in the summer of 2011, when S&P even downgraded the U.S. government debt, though truth be told, they did provide multiple warnings.

CREDIT ANALYSIS: NECESSARY, NOT OPTIONAL

I cannot begin to tell you how many times I have been asked why there is a need for credit analysis when the rating agencies have already rated most of the outstanding debt. Another popular question is why there is a need for ongoing analysis. I cringe every time these questions arise. Maybe, just maybe, I can understand why an investor may have asked the question before 2006, though I still, wouldn't have agreed with the notion that it wasn't needed even then. With that said, after 2007 and all the issues that hit the market around bond ratings, including downgrades, neither one of these questions should have to be asked again. Credit analysis is not optional; it is a necessity in managing a fixed income portfolio. Unless you are buying sovereign debt, analysis of the company should be executed before the trade. There can even be an argument made that analysis of the country and its government is needed, with all that is happening on the political front. My rule of thumb: If it's not a Treasury security, credit work should be done in conjunction with the work from the rating agencies. The analysts on my team may not want to hear that, for the simple reason that it increases the number of holdings they need to cover. The need for credit work should not be driven by the type or structure of the account, either. A separate account structure in a mutual fund credit analysis is a necessity. Active or passive strategy, the credit process is all the same—it needs to be done.

CREDIT FOR A PASSIVE STRATEGY

In a low-turnover or passive strategy, credit is more important than you may think. Credit analysis is the backbone to a laddered or low-turnover strategy. In any portfolio, an asset manager does not want to introduce poor credit into the portfolio; doing so is a recipe for disaster. An active strategy, however, can handle the increased volatility of an unplanned sale and potential loss due to the nature of the strategy. The impact of a loss to a laddered account is quite different. The introduction of poor credit into a passive strategy can be detrimental to its success. A loss doesn't necessarily mean a default. Let's be clear on that. A loss is as simple as buying a bond at par, which is equal to 100, and having to sell it at 98; the classic buy-high and sell-low scenario. If you think about it, in a low-turnover strategy that doesn't include active trading, it is very difficult to make up for any loss that is taken. The size of the loss is critical. A small loss on a percentage basis to the portfolio will over time be recaptured from the coupon stream. The impact will be less income to reinvest or use for activities. A larger loss, in the case of a default, has the potential to ruin the portfolio, and in some circumstances the portfolio may never recover the lost amount. This is because the strategy is not developed to capture capital gains through trading. The strategy is designed and implemented to preserve capital and create a solid income stream.

There are also misconceptions that find their way across my desk on the need to analyze credits that are linked to a government entity. In other words, securities that are supported by or look toward the government for backing. Earlier, I mentioned not having to do credit work on U.S. Treasury securities, and I stand by that statement. However, other securities, including certificates of deposit (CDs) and those that carry some form of lifeline, need to be reviewed. As a result of the most recent financial crisis, many banks and financial institutions found themselves tethered to their government, having needed a lifeline to stay afloat. We have seen a number of banks need to be bailed out here in the United States, as well as overseas. For the most part, the majority of banks that at one time needed a hand from the U.S. government have repaid most or all of the funding received. The ties are severed. All the problems that have happened and continue in Europe have had a longer and lasting impact on certain financial institutions. There are banks that continue to be owned in part by overseas governments. In some regards, this is good for them; at least it was when the markets were spiraling out of control and they needed help. What remains problematic is trying to figure out the most effective way to analyze those companies. One way is to put your full faith in the government and say it will not let anything happen to the entity—it saved them once and will do it again. This is not always the case. Many asset managers and investors alike learned a lesson back in 2008 when the government orchestrated the rescue of Bear Stearns, but stayed out of the way of Lehman Brothers. This is a perfect example of inconsistent activity. The ongoing problem is trying to pin down the government's next move. In theory, this should not be an arduous process. Government activity should be easily communicated and straightforward, similar to a company. What about the political side of the equation? Here is where the problem lies. I find it very difficult to anticipate the next move any government might make. This difficulty escalates even further in the midst of uncertainty. The fear is when the government will say enough is enough. There is a low probability on that trade, but it is possible. I would hate to have to explain why I invested in a security with a reason of "well, I thought the government would stand behind the name." That is just not a good decision for many reasons. The challenge of analysis on government support creeps in more than you may think. Many sectors have to deal with the day-to-day headlines and concerns about the government support of, for instance, a bank.

The money market sector, the front end of the curve with the shortest maturities and lowest perceived risk, embodies certain commercial paper issues that are or were supported by government credit. A sister to traditional financial commercial paper is the asset-backed commercial paper (ABCP) sector. This type of paper usually has a sponsor or provider, typically a bank. If the bank needed to be bailed out in the crisis, guess who is likely part owner? That's right, the government. If the debt, regardless of the type or maturity, is highly rated due to support from the government, how should that be viewed? This is where the dilemma lies. Whether the security is commercial paper or a longer-dated corporate note, a full credit analysis needs to be performed on both the institution and the government as a stand-alone entity. Analysis on a government may sound a bit silly or odd; however, government debt has been recently tested, and discussions on debt to gross domestic product (GDP) and austerity measures are in financial headlines each and every day. Banks that have received government intervention are even found playing in the front end of the municipal market. In some cases, variable-rate demand obligations have a letter of credit from a financial institution, normally a bank, that helps the municipal security achieve its triple-A credit rating. No matter what market you are investing in, you may not be able to get away from the difficult situation of having to make the dreaded call. That call is to possibly choose not to invest in a company due to the support it has from its local government, in essence betting against, or at least not with, the government.

AFTER THE INITIAL APPROVAL

It's not uncommon for rating agencies to issue multiple upgrades and down-grades over the years. Let's be honest; with the recent turbulent markets it may not take years—dramatic activity can happen within months. Other activity includes positive and negative outlooks, which usually—but not invariably—precede an upgrade or downgrade. These positive and negative opinions toward a company influence the markets, and most importantly, investor sentiment. The impact doesn't affect all investors in the same way. These different views and interpretations from investors are what make a market.

Take an automotive company. For discussion purposes, the credit carries a single-A rating. The company has performed very well over the past four quarters, selling 15 percent more cars each quarter than forecast. The company used the additional money to repair its balance sheet by increasing cash reserves and paying down debt. These actions are positive, and the rating agency takes notice of this. Due to the positive growth and responsible actions, the rating agency could take action and release a statement showing their opinion. When there are positive remarks from the agency, it will usually issue an upgrade. The opinion changes the rating of the company by raising the rating up the credit rating food chain. In the case of our auto manufacturer, the rating goes from a single-A to double-A. Are all bonds rated created or rated equal? Of course they aren't. The rating agencies provide the market with a scale; however, it is important to remember that not all double-A bonds are created or should be considered equal. This is a key piece of the puzzle to remember. Upgrades and downgrades happen across the entire credit scale. It doesn't just apply to double-A bonds, but single-A or triple-B as well.

NOT ALL BONDS ARE EQUAL

It is important to remember that all double-A bonds are not created equal. Staying with the auto manufacturer example, as a result of increased auto sales and proper debt management, the auto manufacturer was given an upgrade. Let's say this company produces domestic automobiles. This company is making the right decisions, running its business well. As a result, the company's recently issued debt is performing well. Investors like what they see, ratings have improved, and the spread on its debt is tightening. Investors and individuals at the company are happy. As expected, there are other auto companies in the marketplace. These companies are large and small, and carrying different ratings across the scale. There is a foreign car maker that is also rated double-A. Although both these companies carry the same rating, their credit profiles may be as different as night and day. The foreign auto maker is doing well; however, its sales are starting to slow. It seems to be burning through its cash on hand at a quicker pace than the industry average. The company just brought to the market a new issue that was not very well received by investors. The company was able to issue the entire amount it was looking to issue, so it is fair to say that the deal did okay. The concern was that in order to get the deal done, the dealers and the company had to cheapen the issue to make it more attractive. Is this the end of the world? No, but it is a red flag. This type of activity should be looked at as an early sign from investors that the company may be in store for a rough patch. As a result, there could be some impending rating action. If nothing else, it is a clear signal to investors and credit analysts that the company should be given another look to make sure the current ratings are appropriate. Look at it this way: If the analysis is completed and the view is that the company should maintain the current rating and not be downgraded, then the deal that just came to market at cheaper levels should look attractive. The spread should, over time, tighten in to the company's peers—in this example, to that domestic auto market.

It is not only important to know the fundamentals of the company, such as all the financial ratios needed to hold a solid view. It is also imperative to use common sense. For instance, when we were in the middle of the banking crisis in 2008, it goes without saying that financial institutions were in trouble for multiple reasons. The biggest risk, in my view, was that it was very difficult to get to the bottom of their balance sheets. You just couldn't say with 100 percent certainty that you knew the extent of everything that company was holding. That is a big problem. These institutions could be rated single-A or maybe even double-A. Here is where the common sense kicks in. There are a vast number of nonfinancial names that may be rated comparable to the financial institution discussed above, or possibly even rated lower. Take, for instance, an industrial name that is rated triple-B. This company is still well within the investment-grade universe. This company that is triple-B is a consumer staple, and pretty straightforward in its business. The business model is easy to understand, the components needed to produce the goods are easy to understand. To me, this type of company is easier to analyze. What this is also is telling me is that this triple-B industrial credit carries less risk than the single-A financial institution.

I have said it before and will say it again: always be aware of your surroundings. The credit environment is no exception. It has the potential to throw you a curve ball, surprising you and catching you off guard. Just as the economic and market environment possesses the potential to surprise investors, ratings agencies have the same ability. Catching investors off guard is the best way to create havoc within their portfolio. There is always the daily downgrade in which some are clear and very predictable, others not so much. The lesson here is not to become complacent. If you allow complacency to set in, hold on—you will likely be in for a bumpy ride. That is when the fun begins. There is always the possibility for a series of downgrades to happen in a short amount of times. Contrary to common belief, multiple downgrades have been known to happen. There have been past times when a mass downgrade occurred. This happened within the residential mortgage-backed securities (RMBS) market when thousands of securities were downgraded. If nothing else, multiple downgrades will roil the markets. Volatility will increase and uncertainty will pick up. There may not be a direct impact on your portfolio, but there may be an indirect implication.

Credit analysis doesn't just occur prior to entering into a trade and it shouldn't stop once the trade tickets are confirmed with the dealers and the portfolio manager is focusing on the next trade. Credit analysis is an ongoing requirement. We know and have seen in action that the markets are always changing, as are the debt instruments that we invest in. Whether the change is from developing economic situations or balance sheet decisions, changes do occur and need to be followed. The ongoing review or surveillance on credits that are held within the portfolio allows the credit analyst and overall process to remain proactive. The ability to remain proactive and nimble also helps the portfolio management team stay ahead of the curve and provides them with the ability to take advantage of the dislocation that emerges, which in the end will benefit the portfolio.

STAY AHEAD OF THE HERD

The ability to stay ahead of the herd of investors and markets is paramount to achieve success. It is unlikely that this can be accomplished 100 percent of the time, as it is a difficult task. You just need to achieve success more times than not. Another way to look at this is that your decisions need to be right more often than wrong. In addition, the wrong decisions need to be controlled. An error on a large scale is catastrophic to the portfolio. That notion is sometimes a lot harder than it sounds. Without credit analysis, it becomes even more difficult. This is why credit analysis is instrumental in portfolio management. As I have discussed, analysis should be done within every asset class. Consistent work is the number one goal, although the type of analysis may differ slightly due to the sector under review. This is okay and to be expected. A money market security needs to be analyzed with a heightened focus on liquidity and the company's ability to receive adequate overnight or short-term funding. Tail risk needs to be measured through event-driven scenarios such as if there were a run on the bank assets. For a longer-term corporate position, the analysis may focus more on the company's overall fundamentals, including product pipeline and how the company controls costs, to name a few.

What about the government-insured market—in particular the Federal Deposit Insurance Corporation (FDIC)-insured certificates of deposit (CDs)? Since the financial crisis in 2008, the FDIC CD sector has not been the same. We know that the principal investment is protected up to the stipulated limits by insurance from the government program. With that said, the first questions I am always asked is if that is the case why is there the need for credit analysis? The answer is simple, but probably overlooked by many. First, a little background. Direct and brokered CDs drew heavy interest from investors throughout the recent banking crisis. Fueling the fire was the onslaught of bank closures, which placed significant pressure on the insurance of these certificates. Even with all the pressure and investors that tapped the program, it held up.

Up to this point, we have discussed the role of credit analysis in protecting the portfolio from declines. Now it is time to turn the tables and focus on how credit analysis provides upside potential to a passive account. That statement in itself is counterintuitive when the goal of a ladder or passive account is stability, preservation of capital, and income. Now add into the mix an asset class that carries insurance to protect the principal from a decline in value from a default or bank seizure. If the account is not designed to generate alpha, or capital gains, and to top it off, the securities held in the account are insured by FDIC insurance, why is credit analysis needed? Here is a perfect example of how a portfolio benefits from a watchful eye. I had under management a position in a brokered CD of a particular bank. It was purchased at par; therefore there was not a premium paid on the security. The par amount was well within the limit covered by the FDIC insurance, so there was nothing to be concerned about. After owning the security for roughly a year and a half, my analyst came to me and said that the Fed had just issued a prompt corrective action to this particular bank. Broadly speaking, what that means is that the bank has a set number of days to raise additional capital, and if it doesn't, there is a strong likelihood that the bank will be forced to shut down. There are two paths that we could have taken. The first is probably the more common, which would have been to look to the FDIC insurance to provide payment of the principal and call it a day. The second path, the less traveled, was to go out to the market and try to get a bid on these securities. The thought was straightforward. We should at a minimum get a par bid with the hope of receiving something north of that. Anything north or above par would result in a gain on the security. If the bid would be below par we wouldn't hit it, or in case we weren't even shown a bid, we would accept that fact knowing the CD carried FDIC insurance. After reaching out to a handful of dealers, we received a bid back and it was above par, so naturally we hit the bid and booked the gain. If not for the initial credit work, as well as the ongoing work of following the bank that issued the CD, we might have missed the prompt corrective action, which put in motion the chain of events that resulted in this case. It is a good day when there is a gain on a CD, or any security for that matter, where the bank that issued the note was set to be closed down.

This is a great example of why credit analysis is so very important in every type of strategy. Credit analysis is done for two primary reasons: first, to protect the portfolio from deteriorating credits where loss in principal is possible, and second, to exploit the dislocations within the marketplace in efforts to create gains. The securities in the example were FDIC-insured, so the principal was guaranteed (unless the government entity decided not to make payment). This situation highlights that credit analysis provides the portfolio manager with an opportunity to generate increased profits that would have otherwise been unrealized.

CHAPTER 14

The Four Pillars
of Trade Execution

Price is what you pay. Value is what you get.

—Warren Buffett

As with many things, there is always more beneath the surface when it comes to trading and managing portfolios. Fixed income, equity, swaps and alternatives—it applies to any security in any asset class. The details will just be slightly different from security to security. Let's take a step away from the sexy side of trading fixed income securities. That's right, fixed income has a sexy side. Everyone aspiring to make it in the business wants to be a portfolio manager. It's all glory, right? You always hear about famous investment managers having a great year or making the correct call to avoid the next catastrophe. The rush is always there. At the end of each day, you should know how you and your portfolios are doing. Are you outperforming your benchmark or underperforming, and why? These points are all true. But there is another side and these points do not always occur. In order to achieve your goals, after you put all your hours in on strategizing and security selection, you need to focus on another less-glamorous piece. I am talking about the physical activity of placing the trade. Strategy and modeling aside, there is much more to think about than just pulling the trigger on the trade. (Or in this day and age, tapping the "execute" button on your electronic trading system.) You need to think about the execution of the trade. This is where I narrow the field and think about the four pillars of trading. These pillars are not created for discussion or trade analysis but are reminders of what to think about when trading. These points can also be used as a posttrade checklist to assess your activity. This is actually a very important piece of the system. Analysis of the data is essential to fully capture the benefit of the pillars.

The four pillars of trade execution are

1. Executed price
2. Dealer inquiries
3. Liquidity
4. Ease of transaction

These are the pillars I use when trading investment-grade fixed income securities in the cash market. They are not set in stone. I chose these based on the combination of my industry experience, judgment, and perseverance. You may find it necessary to have six pillars or, maybe only two. Six might be overkill. I don't say this too often, but at that level you will be wasting many hours that could be spent on the sexy part of the job, analyzing and strategizing your next trade. The most important point to remember is that you just need to think about them, plain and simple. Also remember, if you are not managing your money, if you have outsourced your fixed income portfolios, you should ask the manager if he or she not only subscribes to this theory, but implements a process that covers all aspects of investing.

The goal is to take into account the four factors that have the highest impact to provide the best possible trade execution. At one time, trade execution was looked at as receiving the best possible bid or offer from a dealer. In my opinion, that alone is not enough to cover trade execution. It is common for any investment manager to send trades to multiple dealers in an attempt to ensure that the account is provided with a solid picture of the market. On a side note, if you or the manager you hired are only purchasing securities off an inventory page or utilizing a minimal amount of broker-dealers, the best advice I can provide is to find a new manager or broaden your scope.

The use of multiple dealers for assessing market depth is a step in the right direction, but the process shouldn't stop there. Once you collect the data, don't just forget about it. This is where managers lose sight of the big picture and go astray. If you are taking the time to ask the questions and collect the data, take the time to review them. Look for trends or patterns. This may help you become more efficient, and your trades more effective. The more effective and efficient you become, the better execution you will likely receive. This best execution will help you build a better portfolio. Let's dive a little deeper and take a closer look at the four pillars of trade execution.

THE FIRST PILLAR: EXECUTED PRICE

The first pillar, trade execution, is pretty straightforward. When placing a trade, you want to ensure that you are receiving the best possible price. It is not a characteristic that encompasses only one side of the trade. The buy- and sell side transactions are equally important. Think of it like taking a picture. Capture one snapshot at a time, but don't lose sight of the bigger picture. It should go without saying that you must compare like transactions; compare apples to apples. There are a couple of items to remember when comparing prices. First, let's define what the components are that drive the actual price. Not all trades are equal or carry an equal weighting.

The size of the trade is very important. You may see a slightly different price for varying size trades. There is not a set rule; trade size can benefit or hinder the investor depending on the surrounding circumstances such as time of day the trade is placed and even the actual day. For example, if you are trying to buy a bond with a par amount of $500K, you may receive a higher price than if you were looking to buy a block of bonds. Why is this? A broker-dealer's institutional trading desks trade in round blocks. A round lot generally is looked at as a $1 million or $5 million trade. This holds true when investing in the new issue calendar. Don't even bother contacting your sales coverage on a new deal if you are not going in for, or showing interest in, an order of at least $1 million. I am not saying that your coverage will never grant you a favor and allocate a smaller size to you; it is just a harder conversation to have. If you are looking for a smaller size, what usually happens is that after the debt is issued and open for trading, the dealer will offer you some of the deal, either at a new issuer price or slightly different. There is an exception to this rule. When trading, if there is an offering of $5,350,000, the $350,000 is known in the fixed income world as a tail. You can even break the trade up a step further and say that the $50,000 is known also as a tail. Usually the dealer will be more than happy to sell you that $50, 000 or $350,000 at the same price or sometimes at a better price than the round lot. At first glance it looks as if the dealer is doing you a favor. That may be true, but what is also happening and the reason why they are willing to enter into this trade is to clean up their books. Or another way to look at it is that the dealer wants to hold all round positions. It is the traditional give-take relationship that in the end benefits both parties. The investor is happy because he or she purchased a bond below current market price, instantly creating a position that is in the money. The party on the other end of the trade is happy because you just helped them clean up their books and reduce balance sheet risk. Granted, it may be hard to find out the overall position that the dealer has or is willing to sell. The amount of difficulty depends on the relationship the asset manager has with the firm he or she is trading with.

Trade size also matters when you are looking to sell bonds. This side of the trade is a bit more complicated. The environment and timing weigh heavily. If you are looking for a bid on an odd lot position (not a round lot), the bid you will likely receive will show a haircut. That is a price below current market price. The dealer or individual on the other end of the trade is likely going to be less willing to show you a strong bid. It is all relative—the bid from the investor perspective is softer than you would be expecting, but the dealer probably feels like they are doing you a favor by taking these bonds off your hands. When it comes to timing, it is common that you receive a poorer bid or price late in the day. This doesn't always happen, but if the trader at the dealer is getting ready to close her books for the day, he or she may not be as interested in buying your bonds. If the end of the day is a poor time to trade, take a step back and think about how problematic selling into a long holiday weekend would be. It makes perfect sense, but unfortunately common sense is not followed. As an asset manager, if not requested, I would not go to the market and look for a bid on a bond during the three days leading up to a holiday. The problem is that end investors have a habit of spending money in the holiday season. This happens every year, but with a little planning, it can be avoided. Trying to sell a position to raise cash before a holiday is just not a good idea. It can be accomplished; however, the end result is frequently not as pleasant an experience as expected. Markets are usually thin on holiday weeks; there is less activity, and bid-ask spreads have a tendency to widen. Backup traders are usually manning the posts and very hesitant to add any positions to the balance sheet. Month-end and holidays, the Street is usually looking to derisk their books, and adding to positions contradicts that goal. By raising cash one week earlier, the holiday is in all interested parties' sights, but still far enough in the distance not to create a handicap on the trade. Just keep that in mind.

If you are looking to allocate additional funds to a portfolio, it may be in your best interest to do so in that same time frame. In past years I have found it very advantageous to go on buying sprees leading up to holiday breaks. For similar reasons dealers don't want to add exposure to the balance sheet, they are willing to reduce the exposure as well. Negotiations on prices have a tendency to move more smoothly with greater benefits to the portfolio. If you can remember these facts when trading or raising cash for your clients, you will be ahead of the game. Every little bit counts when entering a trade. There are many outside influences that you don't have control over, which is why it is so important to capitalize on those pieces that you do.

THE SECOND PILLAR: DEALER INQUIRIES

Pillar number 2 covers the importance of dealer inquiries and why you should be concerned. As a fiduciary to client portfolios, this is a topic of interest that should be discussed at some point with your team. Regardless if this topic becomes a conversation piece for you or turns into one of your pillars, it is an area that you should be educated about and at a minimum familiar with. This question is suitable for anyone who is involved in the market. If you and your portfolios are not benefiting from the access to multiple dealers you are harming the portfolio.

Just for a moment, let's say that you have an unlimited number of dealers that you can utilize. The first question you might ask is, how many should I use? How many should a trade be directed to? Is there a different number for buy tickets versus sell tickets? I am always asked what the magic number is. The short answer is, well, that depends. At that point the response is as if I have three heads. "It depends" is a valid and strong answer. Different types of trading or trading in various sectors may require more or less dealer inquiries. Why the variation? At the end of the day, you need to feel that you are provided a fair representation of the market. For example, trying to sell a Treasury note is completely different from selling a municipal bond or debt issued within the high-yield market. The Treasury market is one of the most liquid, if not the most liquid, market with transparency that is easily witnessed. The more transparent the market, the easier it is to see the market and daily price activity. Having the ability to feel confident about the market gives you the comfort that the portfolio received a fair price.

The municipal market is a great example of a market that is less transparent. The lack of transparency creates the potential for greater price discrepancy. If you ever had the chance to review trade history at the security level, you would notice that certain municipal debt doesn't trade on a regular basis. Many asset managers buy municipal debt, lock it up, and throw away the key. The lack of transactions creates pricing inefficiencies. There is a chance to exploit the dislocations within the market if you have the ability to source debt through multiple dealers. The fact that the market is less efficient also creates the need for additional research.

When all is said and done, the number of dealers that should be used is whatever number that makes you feel comfortable that the trade was executed at an acceptable price. The liquidity of different sectors ranges from Treasuries—the most liquid—to credit and municipal debt, which are a little more complicated. The rule of thumb is the lower the credit quality or the more infrequently a bond trades, the less transparent it will be and the need for additional dealers is likely.

THE THIRD PILLAR: LIQUIDITY

The third pillar is liquidity. We discussed liquidity earlier in this book; now let's look at it from another angle. Liquidity has another meaning, particularly when it revolves around two different parties that are involved in the issuance of new debt. Any time a new issue is brought to the market, the first questions that need to be asked and discussed are: Who is the underwriter going to be on the deal? Who was involved in the initial sale of the bonds? Also, who was in charge of billing and delivering? These are three distinct and very important questions. Right now, your next questions are probably be why is this important and how do I find this information out?

To start, it is important because it ties back into the common definition of liquidity. The more dealers that are involved in issuing the debt, the better liquidity the bonds should have. The number of dealers involved in the deal is important because they will likely be more willing to put a bid on the bond when needed. The reason for this is that they are more familiar with the debt because they were involved in some form of conception. Whether it was in the underwriting process, booking process, or just the selling process, the bottom line is that they should be comfortable with the deal. This comfort level will create additional liquidity. If there is an increase in liquidity, there is a greater chance of receiving multiple bids for your bonds, which should translate into a better price. Think of it this way: if there is only one dealer on the issue, the dealers have the advantage. The competitive market has just been transformed into a market where one player has all the information at hand and the others don't; there is a slight advantage favoring the one with knowledge. The easiest way you can find this information is from the sales coverage on the deal. Market systems such as Bloomberg terminals also store and provide the data, as well as the offering statement. This type of research and analysis should be innate to a credit analyst.

THE FOURTH PILLAR: EASE OF TRANSACTION

The final pillar is very straightforward, as straightforward as the first pillar of executed price. Ease of transaction is the most simplistic pillar to assess and yet is still very important. Although this sounds like common sense, if there is a breakdown in the process, it could cause insurmountable havoc. When executing a trade, ask yourself, was the transaction easy to accomplish? Were you able to execute the trade without any problems? Did the trade settle properly? All easy but serious questions that you should think of every time you place a trade. A problem could be as simple as, if trading electronically, did the online site crash during your trade? Was it slow in processing the trade? If you have outsourced management, these questions should be asked. Dive deep into the discussion. Don't just settle for the standard "of course we do." Ask for examples and what happens if scenarios occur and how they monitor the activity. These are all questions that you may take for granted and not even think about, but you should.

I always am amazed when a dealer is offering a position—let's say $5,000,000 for this example. You took the time to do your homework and feel comfortable with the bond and the trade. The price is fair and you are looking to purchase the entire $5,000,000 block. When you click the execute button or fill button, the message you receive is that these bonds are no longer available. You pick up the phone and press the representative to fill your order, but the deal must have just been sold. The bottom line is that it doesn't matter whether the bonds were actually just sold; if they have not been purchased by you and are not in your account. This is easy to stomach if it just happens once, or maybe even twice. Multiple times is just not acceptable. If working with an asset manager, the response would be somewhat different. The first answer from your sales coverage might be similar. It was a bad post; the bonds sold. The next question out of my mouth would, be what are you going to do now? Are you going to short the position and sell me what was offered? Or are you going to go out through your sources and find me the bonds or an equivalent issue? In either situation, you now have a headache on your hands. It is likely that you will spend more time trying to resolve this issue then you spent analyzing the bond. This is just an example, and this exact situation may never happen to you. But even if this particular case doesn't arise, another one may, and you want to make sure that you are aware of the situation so you can navigate through the issues and come out ahead. If this sort of thing does happen, how are you going to handle it? It is prudent to keep a record. Keep track of all the failed trades that occur. Make sure that in the notes, a record is kept of which party created the failed trade. When analyzing your approved broker-dealers, if there are reoccurring offenders, my suggestion would be to remove them from your approved list and move on. Utilize the shops that are just as concerned about trade execution as you (or your asset manager) are. The Street is not shy of broker-dealers who are ready and willing to open a new account and start a new relationship.

Professional investment managers have a fiduciary responsibility to develop and implement reasonable steps for trade execution, but it doesn't stop there. As mentioned earlier, the process and findings then need to be reviewed and analyzed. The point is: No matter how simple this sounds, it is of the utmost importance, which is why most, if not all, professional money managers have a process and procedures built around this topic.

CHAPTER 15

There Are No Roadblocks, Just Detours

Rule No. 1: Never lose money. Rule No. 2: Never forget rule No. 1.

—Warren Buffett

Early in any asset manager's career, the capital markets teach you two very important lessons. Always know what you own and develop thick skin. Realizing this early in your career could save many hours of second-guessing yourself and ultimately embarrassment.

KNOW WHAT YOU OWN

It is crucial to always know what you own. I don't mean the basics such as the name of the security or bond type and structure. Knowing details at that level is always a given. What I am referring to are the minutiae, every little detail. The characteristic that is the most obscure is the detail that questions will arise from.

It happens to all of us and usually early on in the career. A bond is purchased and the characteristics meet all the specifications required by the portfolio guidelines. This would normally encompass the basic characteristics such as the ratings, structure or type of the bond, sector, and where it fits in the capital structure. That is fine for starters, but incomplete. As the saying goes, the devil is in the details. What differentiates credits and the ability to seek out the winners is uncovering the layers that tell the entire story of the credit. Once the shell is cracked, analyze what lies beneath.

BANKING SECTOR

Let's apply this to the financial sector. It is no surprise that problems are prevalent within this sector. A good asset manager will take advantage of the dislocations when they occur, creating opportunities to purchase, for example, bank debt. He or she will also know when to remain on the sidelines. The difficult part is knowing when to remain out of particular names, even when they may look cheap. The only way to have the ability to make an educated call like this is to do your homework and know what you are looking to buy. All banks are not created equal.

The banking and financial sector in today's environment has more flavors then were ever before imaginable. There are large money center banks, regional banks, and banks that are partially and fully owned by governments. At times it becomes very difficult to separate. One of the most important questions that need to be answered is what does the bank own on its balance sheet and how does the bank capture revenue? Through different forms of analysis, the differentiation of banks will appear. Knowing what the bank owns will ultimately provide you the insight about what you own. Analysis is one area that will foster the development of a sound opinion and view. It makes sense that all banks are not created equal. There are different areas that these institutions may focus on. Some are more tied to the mortgage market as lending is a key component to the business. Others may focus more on the brokerage or capital markets side of the business. There isn't a right or wrong answer; you just need to know the details. If we are in the middle of a mortgage crisis, common sense tells you that banks that are heavily involved in the mortgage market will likely be trading cheaper. Other banks may follow the trend of trading cheaper in sympathy, even though they are not tied, or have minimal exposure to, the mortgage market. This anomaly of credits trading in sympathy happen as investors shed risk to the overall sector. Spreads may also widen if the bank carries the perception that it is involved in the mortgage market. A lower credit rating, or even a less well-known name, may also initially drive spreads wider and cause underperformance. The only way to get your arms around the bond is to do your homework.

It should make absolute sense that the bond trading lower in sympathy probably makes much more sense to purchase, even if it is not as well known or it carries a lower rating. On the surface, the lower-rated smaller bank might look riskier; however, after analysis, your view might change. Ultimately, the bank involved in the mortgage sector may have further to decline if the mortgage crisis deepens. If this sector continues to reprice lower, it is immaterial if the bank is partially or fully owned by the government. Investors will take a risk-controlled approach and shy away from the name or at the very least demand a larger haircut for the debt. The full picture takes time to uncover. It usually doesn't just appear and present itself. What you will find is that if you do your homework with specific analysis at both the company and macro level, a clear differentiation will emerge from the problem credits and those moving in sympathy. As the saying goes, the devil is in the details, which holds so true with security selection within the fixed income markets

GO WITH YOUR GUT!

Time and time again investors were hit with one obstacle after another. Beginning in 2007, the onslaught of hurdles was relentless. From political uprisings to natural disasters, investors were tested. The end goal was to stimulate the economy, which the central banks made significant progress towards. Figure 15.1 shows the 10-year yield, along with recent headwinds since 2007. The highlighted events represent a few monumental turning points that created a stir within the fixed income world.

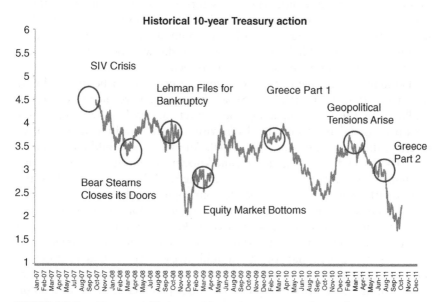

FIGURE 15.1 10-year yield along with turning points in the market
Source: Bloomberg data.

- August 2007: SIV crisis
- March 2008: Bear Stearns shut its doors
- September 2008: Lehman filed for bankruptcy
- March 2009: Equity market bottomed
- First Quarter 2010: Greece, part 1
- First Quarter 2011: Geopolitical tensions, Egyptian president Hosni Mubarak is overthrown
- 2011: Greece, part 2

This list is very diverse with many unthinkable events. Many of these turning points were unpredictable, catching most investors off guard. A few were telegraphed, and markets were able to take precautions. Other situations that were telegraphed still rocked the markets, as investors either looked the other way or figured the unthinkable couldn't happen. After Bear Stearns was acquired by JPMorgan, with help from the government, the Treasury market found a reason to sell off. The world was a better place. Not because Bear Stearns was no longer in existence, but because the government had set a precedent. It had orchestrated the deal with JPMorgan, making a statement that it was a lifeline if firms found themselves in trouble. Investors in the masses believed this; whether everyone was drinking the same Kool-Aid, the wall of worry was no longer needed. The next 6 months are history. As soon as Bear Stearns unraveled, the sights were set on Lehman Brothers. At first the markets didn't react the way I would have expected them to. The debt still traded well, and why not? The common view was that if needed, the government would help them out just as it did with Bear Stearns. A few months went by and memories were short-lived.

Lehman management was proclaiming everything to be fine and that there was nothing to worry about. Slowly but surely, more and more negative headlines hit the tape, impacting the markets as a whole, and Lehman's stock price and debt specifically. Even with negative headline after negative headline, the stock and debt traded well. All investors should have taken a step back, looked at the big picture, and known something was wrong. This was not the first time the writing was on the wall. If you look back to the prior months before Enron and WorldCom imploded, the markets provided warning sings. Cheap debt levels and ongoing rumors were some of the warning signs that just could not be overlooked. Even if taken with a grain of salt, the salt pile starts to build until there is a mound of trouble. There were so many red flags that your gut should have told you to take your money and run. Leading up to the weekend before the Lehman bankruptcy papers were filed, the stock price fell from 16.30 on September 2, 2008, to 3.65 on September 12. This move telegraphed what was about to occur, ultimately leading to the price of 21 cents on Monday, September 15. The short-term debt prior to that Friday, September 12 traded at ridiculous levels: high double-digit yields for very short-term paper that matured within a few days. What topped it off was the Friday before the company filed for bankruptcy, when I called over to the sales desk in the early afternoon to inquire what levels Lehman debt was trading at. I spoke to the sales coverage that picked up the phone and they said that the desk wasn't trading any more that day. This was at around 1:00 P.M. First off, a trading desk usually welcomes a possible trade, particularly early in the afternoon. After 5:30 P.M, they may hesitate, sure, but not at 1:00 P.M. There was a fabricated excuse that just didn't add up. You could tell that the individual was uncomfortable and it seemed that he had been provided with a script that day to faithfully communicate. It was something like the company was trying to close their books and settle up for the day. It should have been clear that it was trying to settle up for eternity. If the free fall in the equity price and the double-digit yields somehow passed your gut test, which I don't know how they would, the fact that the trading desk was closing early for the day should have signaled that the ship was sinking. That was the mother of all red flags. The bottom line is, you must trust your instinct and go with your gut.

If it doesn't smell right, just stay away. It makes sense to remove yourself from the situation, even though it might only be temporary. If that is the case, during the time you are sidelined, you are an observer assessing the new developments, making a decision whether or not to get back in. My rule of thumb in times of uncharacteristically high uncertainty is that it is better to hit the bid, reassess the situation, and determine if you want to be involved—and if so, at what level. Remaining disciplined to the process is what sets managers apart.

DON'T TAKE IT PERSONALLY

There will always—and I mean *always*—be a naysayer or someone who will take a different view from yours. There is always going to be someone who disagrees with you and the decisions that you are making. Remain confident in what you do and embrace the challenge. That is what makes a market. Monday morning quarterbacks are not uncommon in the asset management industry. Think about it: It is very easy for someone to question a view, call, or even a trade that you put on, particularly if it is out of the money.

Managing money is not about trading a book of securities. The trades that you place are usually implemented for the long haul. That time frame may be defined differently depending on who you ask. Regardless of how it is defined, be prepared, at some point, to be underwater. If and when that is the case, the critics will emerge. It is not uncommon, because one day your trade may be out of the money, the next day, back in. The move may be driven by fundamental reasons or an exogenous event that could not possibly have been predicted. Whatever the reason or rationale for the move, if the homework was done, you should be confident in every trade entered. Don't follow the tick-by-tick analysis; remember that your trade is entered for the long term. Develop your thick skin early on in your career. You will be tested and questioned many times over. In the end if you have a thesis for the trade, that is your reason, and at an expected exit point, pull the trigger. Whatever comes down the road afterwards, don't take it personally.

TRAPPED IN PURGATORY

There is no better way to describe the fixed income environment over recent years than "fixed-income purgatory." The dizzying environment has made most days feel as if they were Groundhog Day. The market opens and trades in one direction before reversing course mid-day and finishing either off the highs or lows. The relentless news about global dislocations, geopolitical woes, and hopes of a recovery has created a range-bound environment across multiple asset classes and across the yield curve. Over time, the range has shifted lower as the fixed income bull market, driven in part by investor fear and central bank intervention, has produced historic low yields. Immunity is not an option, as the front-end money market instruments, credit sector, and the municipal sector have all felt the pain.

If asked precrisis where Treasury levels would be in five years, most would have found it hard to believe that the fed funds rate would be close to zero, with Treasury bill yields negative and a 10-year trading at times below 1.5 percent. It is difficult to get your arms around this unprecedented activity, and if asked, most investors would agree that these types of yields were unsustainable. Therefore, these levels are hard to believe. These levels are representative of a different time. Markets have changed, as did the economic landscape. Pure panic was the initial driver as investors had to digest in 2008 and 2009 that the economy and financial systems were on the threshold of a complete meltdown. We know that there are times when the tone of both the economy and markets shifts on a dime from feeling healthier than the levels during the crisis to spiraling downward out of control. Panic mode in investors' psyche has subsided. Replacing the panic is the ongoing uncertainty.

At this stage in a recovery there is the expectation that interest rates would be higher by now. The opposite has occurred; the recovery has continued to fuel Treasury prices higher. Timing may be slower than expected as different parts of the yield curve are artificially anchored through central bank activity. Without the intervention, the expectation is that Treasury yields would be at least 75 to 100 basis points higher than where they stand within the current cycle. This move has had difficulty materializing, even as the bond bears relentlessly try to push yields higher every time there is a whiff of inflation or stronger-than-expected rhetoric from market figureheads. In the blink of an eye, the moves lower are met with significant headwinds, pushing prices higher and driving yields lower. The battle between global growth and global sovereign debt concerns will continue for many years to come. The sovereign debt battle will morph from one country to another, frequently taking on new shapes. The headwinds and obstacles will continue to test investors and asset managers alike as we move through the years.

The global turmoil within the markets impacting fixed income investors has taken years to develop. There is no doubt that it will take even longer to work its way fully out of the system. After the headwinds abate, the environment will feel much healthier and calmer, and the market will function normally while investors wait for the next disruption. Not to sound too negative, but there will be another disruption to address.

We have covered a substantial amount of information on navigating within the fixed income market. Fixed income markets should not remain in a black hole, and neither should your investment strategy or portfolio. Going forward, any turmoil or dislocations should be met with courage and knowledge to succeed. You have the tools to create and execute the appropriate strategy in any environment. The bull market will eventually meet with resistance and the markets will pose challenges. Remember that there are many headwinds that pop up when investing within the fixed income universe. These headwinds should be viewed only as minor detours and not as roadblocks. A solid road map and game plan will allow you to navigate successfully through any environment. Trust yourself and your instincts!

Index

Printed and bound by CPI Group (UK) Ltd, Croydon, CR0 4YY

16/04/2025

14658446-0001